# Cultivating the Hospitable Mind

Dr Leon van Achterbergh

There are very few things in life that satisfy me more than seeing my students perform optimally in the workplace. I relish the praises from their line managers and never fail to feel proud of their well-earned achievements.

I dedicate this book to them. They have taught me as much as I have had the privilege to teach them. I look forward to them evolving into future captains of the hospitality industry.

Published by New Generation Publishing in 2019

Copyright © Dr Leon van Achterbergh 2019

First Edition

www.newgeneration-publishing.com

Book design and production ready for print Keith Hodgsonat Ant Creative keith@antcreative.com www.antcreative.com.

ISBN 978-1-78955-439-7

# FOREWORD

A couple of years ago, my wife and I were in Cyprus at an independent hotel in the center of Nicosia. We had arrived early evening and tired after the flight we decided to have dinner in the hotel. It was about 7.30 p.m. by the time we entered an empty restaurant. The only other diner had just finished her meal. We chose a table (there were plenty) and the waiter gave us the menus. Not surprisingly, there was no atmosphere. The other guest mentioned as she passed our table that they also served roughly the same menu in the bar, which was a modern, more intimate space with large picture windows letting in the evening light. Apologising to the waiter for deserting him, we headed for the bar and found a nice table in the window. A lot more pleasant. Until the barman arrived. We asked for menus. He told us that the restaurant was open and was just across the reception area and we would probably be more comfortable there. We persisted. He brought the menus. Eventually, we ordered. He brought the food. He gave us it. The food was pretty good. The service non-existent. We actually had a thoroughly enjoyable evening, laughing at the barman as every new guest entered and he tried his best to discourage them from staying.

About the same time, a colleague and I visited the newly opened Flat Iron in Convent Garden in London. If you have not come across this concept, they serve a steak and side salad for a very reasonable price, to which you can add sides from a small (but remarkably tasty) selection. Popcorn as an appetiser with your drinks but no starters and no desserts. Only one cut of steak is on the menu – a Flat Iron, not surprisingly – with one alternative, such as a burger, that changes on a daily basis. No bookings. You queue until a table is ready. Our waitress was a delight. She introduced us to the menu and the concept in a friendly, informative and knowledgeable way. She responded to our questions and attempts at humour with good grace and fun. She delivered the steaks and sides efficiently and made sure we were enjoying our experience. We were. She really was very good at what she does. I have been back on numerous occasions and although the staff have changed, their approach and professionalism haven't.

There is no doubt that as a customer you can recognise when the person serving you 'gets it' and conversely when they don't. Getting to the bottom of what makes good hospitality and how to engender that feeling in yourself and in others is much more difficult. This book sets out to help you on a journey of discovery to find the hospitality within you. It is drawn from the insight, learning, observation and experience of one man who will mentor you on that journey. This is not a series of simple steps to service success. This is a thoughtful exploration of what it takes to develop the hospitableness within you and bring it out to delight the people around you. Leon states in one part of the book that his mission is "to educate, mentor and facilitate students, graduates and employees to fully engage with their work and to fulfil their career ambitions in the hospitality industry". This book goes a long way to achieve that mission.

**Prof Andrew Lockwood**

Forte Professor of Hospitality Management, University of Surrey

# FOREWORD

Hospitality is a heavily written about and described subject. It's often associated with a natural gift, or the question if we can actually be taught to be hospitable. "Cultivating the Hospitable Mind" sheds a clear light on many aspects of hospitality, which for sure will provide guidance and insight to improving service. Are there choices to be made in our attitude, or are we governed by our character and upbringing?

At citizenM we have empowered our line staff – "the ambassadors" – fully to be responsible for guest satisfaction. The rest of the organisation simply supports that final delivery. We don't judge or train, we check for alignment of values. The many aspects "Cultivating the Hospitable Mind" raises, allows you to check many elements of your own awareness, which can then be mapped against your service contributions. This intangible aspect about service is already difficult to grasp. When mapped against the environment this required service is even more difficult to bare. Once you have read the book and examined the many valuable aspects, I would suggest allowing the human aspect to prevail… in the end it is about a connection and willingness to serve.

As for my own career, here are some learnings from my experiences:

- Be aligned with the purpose of your employer / hospitality environment; it allows you to be yourself at all times…
- Know and understand all tasks, repeat and repeat again. Like driving a car, you forget to operate the machine and enjoy the outcome… a natural service delivery.
- Service can be delivered one to one, most often it is best done in teams together. Even if you are the star on the team, it is about inclusion and togetherness.
- Give, give and give again, and don't take – this is the name of the game.
- Provide service and don't expect anything in return; anything then coming your way is a plus and bonus.
- Service never ends, it is not a job, it is a way of being. So from waking up at home, delivering professional hospitality, to returning home. It's constant throughout the entire day…
- Don't expect a pat on the back, delivering hospitality is the reward.

I wish you much reading pleasure, as I know you will be triggered and challenged

by the great content of "Cultivating the Hospitable Mind". In the end, however you provide your service, make it natural to you, and sticky to your guest.
Happy serving!

**Michael Levie**
Co-founder and Chief Operations Officer, citizenM Hotels

# INTRODUCTION

Deep in my thirties, whilst working in a hotel lounge in Palestine, I recall watching the 9/11 Twin Towers incident in New York unfold on television. During this arresting broadcast I had to attend, intermediately, to the pending guests' bathrooms, scrubbing grubby toilets, swiftly cleaning them during the few advertisement breaks in the news. This memory became momentous to me for three reasons. Firstly, for the obvious major catastrophe that has since changed the face of global terrorism. Secondly, for the fact that I unwittingly found myself in a fascinating, war-torn part of the Middle-East that held very little future promise in terms of peace, or for that matter, my future prospects. The third reason was the dawning realisation that, just maybe, I wasn't that well suited to the hospitality industry.

Here I was, scrubbing guest toilets in Palestine, as the wider world radically changed. My career aspirations seemed as exciting as the pungent sludge I disposed of down the drain. My sentiments about, and ambitions for, the hospitality industry were barely palatable then. Surviving a chequered past in numerous industries, I'd had my fair share of career lows. I mostly followed the money, taking a route that meandered through a variety of job descriptions. I never really followed a logical plan, although I've since managed to progressively explore my aptitudes and abilities (or lack of) rather well. I was more of an analytical thinker than a practical doer. To be particularly forthright with myself, I regarded myself as more of an observer than an action hero in life. This karmic realisation brought me, later, to embrace higher education as a vocation. I found academia to be as comforting to my system as a well-worn glove: snug, reassuring and warm. I found my purpose: facilitating knowledge, understanding and career growth in others.

In the hospitality industry I faced the behemoth of paradoxes. This is an industry that's ostensibly glamorous. However, its glitter quickly wore off for me. It's conducive to the excesses of the wealthy, but often rather depressing in what it delivers as rewards to the hospitality employee. It's like being the proverbial sidewalk shoe-shiner smartening others' luxurious footwear. You get so close, touching that handstitched leather and working with its splendour. However, you remain far away from the real experience of luxury. As a working professional, you invariably need to manage your involvement, psychologically, by keeping a certain distance. Familiarity is a real danger when attempting to be professional. It is easy to take a step too far in being attentive to customers. Hospitality professionalism follows a fine line in this respect. This fine line will be discussed in more detail during the course of the book.

The hospitality industry often creates a playpark for frivolous consumers, where we make sure all their desires are provided for and that they're amply looked after. The industry feeds monstrous egos, yet requires its hosts to maintain their humility. With the daily tribulations of high-stress hospitality jobs, it's no wonder that many newcomers reconsider their career choices and think of quitting. In the past I have often reflected on my own career, and frequently been in a state of renunciation, trying to convince myself that 'I shouldn't be here'. My chequered past, leaving unwanted jobs, seemed indicative of my reluctance to cope with reality. I rationalised my actions by blaming the incompetence of companies and their likeminded managers. You can easily convince yourself that it's better to leave when situations get tough, and, rather than reflect on personal shortcomings, we often project our insecurities outward. This emerges as the defensive 'I'm right, they are wrong' mindset. Similar emotions occur in our minds when we are required to apologise, and we are unwilling to do so. Later in this book we will say more on how our minds delude us in this way.

However, that day in Palestine, something had changed. Freshly emancipated from disposing of that foul-smelling sludge, I decided there and then that I'd take on this somewhat cruel industry. As unappetising as it appeared then, I decided that I'd persist. Somehow I realised the hospitality industry fascinated me and greatly stimulated my analytical side. This eventually led me towards academia. Gradually getting to know my own limiting attitudes, I felt compelled to guide others in my wake. I've had the good fortune to become instrumental in others' career successes. This has turned out to be the most evolving part of my career, and also the most fulfilling. I have seen others exponentially gain from me sharing my experiences with them.

The interdependency between industry and academia has since formed my professional pursuit. Undoubtedly, hospitality being a challenging career choice, it creates winners and losers like few other industries. To be truly successful you cannot remain mediocre. You will be called upon to exhibit an extraordinary mindset: a hospitable mind. If, as you progress through the ranks, for some reason you decide to not acquire this mindset, you create a good chance of failure. My message is clear: you need to make a conscious 'all or nothing' commitment to fully pursue your hospitality career.

Fifteen years ago this fascination with the industry led me to Switzerland, to complete a Master degree in hospitality and pursue an academic career in hospitality. Furthering my ambitions and credentials, I embarked upon, and attained, my Doctorate in business. Consistently giving pastoral care to university students on industry placement has given me some insight into the ambiguous workings of the hospitable mind, and I have investigated countless 'moments of truth'. My initial fascination with employees' psycho-sociological mindset in serving others has persisted, eventually leading to me to write this book. However, this book doesn't provide magical remedies with unambiguous answers for instant success. Quite the contrary; it aims to be an intimate discussion that stimulates the mind. I have attempted to discuss and clarify typical attitudinal conundrums we face daily. Additionally, the journey you will follow in this book will attempt to clarify much of the uncertainties of career choice. Examples from industry, my own experience, a variety of research and some case studies have been explored to give you a holistic interpretation. Hospitality practitioners are an obvious audience for this book. Most people who participate regularly in the welfare of, or care for, others, should find much value here. The book dispenses some of the necessary information, suggestions, and especially the awareness to realise this seemingly illusive mindset. The content should serve well as a source of career reaffirmation for hospitality and human resource practitioners. Aspiring hospitality students will find much value in reflecting on the issues covered, hopefully discovering some guiding principles about their career purpose. It is not intended to be an academic textbook for the select few.

Thus the value proposition of this book is much wider in scope. All those who read this book are likely to improve their relational approach to humanity. Being aware and mindful of why we are hospitable to others will not just lead to a greater chance of career success, but also highlight the real purpose of why we do what we do in service to others.

There are those naturally gifted individuals who seem to be inexplicably made for facing customers and guests, seemingly having an untainted selfless demeanour and a born talent to serve. They warmly welcome people who are indifferent, they pacify the angry, they charm the surly, and they cosset the socially distant. Customers' fondest memories are often formed from the scintillating impressions left by these gifted individuals. The ostensible skill with which these personal connections are created during service encounters is uncanny. We instinctively know when we're exposed to genuine care and empathy. Somehow it gives us a sense of sublime affinity with the essence of humanity. It is as though we have been recognised at a deeper level. We are seen and appreciated as an equal. One might sense that these hospitable-minded persons have connected to us in some, almost spiritual way. I've always been somewhat in awe of these hospitable qualities, and I have witnessed how these can potentially transform businesses, and individuals' careers, for the better. In fact,

I've learnt that much of the time these qualities can be recognised and developed within the individual.

The question of 'why' we do things should always be a precursor to 'how' we need to do it; we need good reason to pursue our purpose. The reasons for and purposes of wanting to pursue the hospitable mind are clarified in the first chapter, as the theme of 'reliability' suggests. Being reliable illustrates the essence of commitment, and doing things for the right reasons. In the second chapter, we explore how managing your own 'responsiveness' in this industry, by willingly working long hours under frequent stressful conditions, becomes both a personal challenge, as well as a pleasure. What indeed, drives the higher performers to go the extra mile? How does one build the necessary confidence to consistently be effective within the hospitable role? Elements of 'assurance' are explored in the third chapter, where the key competencies are discussed and brought into career context. Assurance is a crucial component when higher levels of trust are formed, in providing excellent service. As purpose is fundamental in all of life's achievements, it can only be effectively maintained by motivation and enthusiasm, especially when things are not going your way. In the fourth chapter our indispensable emotional and mental applications and how they effectually relate to other people will be highlighted. By analysing 'empathy' we will notice how developing our sense of care, as well as our quality of responses to guests, will contribute to a fulfilling career. Finally, in the fifth chapter, we observe how important proper presentation is to professionalism and creating trust. Presentation is widely discussed, from the science of smiling, to portraying our attitudes through our actions. We conclude in the sixth and last chapter by looking at continuous development and improving our outlook throughout our career.

In order to frame the different chapters within this book, I have used the well-known SERVQUAL Model that originated from the academics Parasuraman, Zeithaml and Berry. The five essential service quality components of the model enabled the titles to the first five chapters of this book: reliability, assurance, responsiveness, empathy, and presentation (tangibles). I used these themes merely to discuss my view of their relevance to the hospitable mindset. I haven't referenced specific research as I wanted to make this book non-academic. This will hopefully enable the reader to effectively contemplate their psychological approach to hospitality. The book's content isn't so much directed towards the 'technical methods' style of literature. There are many other practical books well suited to this purpose. I have, rather, attempted to explore the themes of 'how to think about' and 'why you should think this way'. As a final thought, I have attempted to illustrate what I've learnt from the many placement and graduate students I've mentored whilst working in hospitality higher education. This book contains an eclectic combination of philosophical, psychological and hospitality-related dimensions. It collects the total of my experience and knowledge gained over a 30-year career period.

CHAPTER 1

# Being reliable:
# are you acceptant or are you fearful?

*"Service is the rent that we pay for our room on earth."*

**Lord Halifax**

## The essence of hospitality

So what does it mean to be hospitable? At risk of sounding like a typical pompous academic, what is hospitality to the layman? In popular dictionaries it's defined as being friendly and welcoming to visitors or guests. It is also understood as receiving or treating guests or strangers warmly and generously, promising warmth and generosity. It also necessitates the host to be open to, and anticipate, the guest's needs and desires. Such desires might include physiological, social and psychological expectations that need to be fulfilled. We note that certain behaviours present themselves when hosts provide hospitality to guests. These should involve benefits to fulfil both parties' needs. The obvious benefit to hosts is monetary. However, with consistently excellent products and service, the hosts will also benefit from fulfilment of other objectives, which include reputational and market growth. The guests' benefit is amicable recognition and due attention. They are welcomed into a socially secure environment. Additionally the benefits go way beyond the physical transaction of providing a bed or a meal. Service requires the most subtle, intangible processes to enhance guests' experiences, which include feeling welcome, respected, and being provided for with various types of assistance. The way service is perceived by customers ultimately determines their experience of the hospitality provided, and whether their expectations have been met or even exceeded.

To place these fundamentals in perspective, one needs to ponder the so-called 'moment of truth'. Generally, a moment of truth occurs when we experience something or someone that will have a sudden and significant effect on our feelings during and after the encounter. In hospitality, it is this momentary connection between a guest and host that will leave a lasting impression. These valuable connections happen at various points throughout the service process, from the initial personal contact, until long after the consumption has taken place.

So why is this essential for us to know? Whenever we communicate with others, such 'moments of truth' inevitably occur. In fact, moments of truth continuously occur throughout the exchange process. These could include the exchanges of pleasantries, information, opinions or other contact facilitated to build rapport or conclude a deal. These moments provide us with the opportunity to gain the necessary level of trust to make an informed decision. Alternatively, initial unfavourable impressions can also impose disruptive feelings and emotions that could cloud our judgements negatively. When thoughts such as these are non-conducive to the situation, we create mental obstacles for ourselves that make it more difficult to communicate effectively. Prejudices are more likely to manifest.

Whenever you approach your guests with trepidation, prejudice, or resentment, you are most likely to project this negative mindset through your thought processes, which precede any associated action that you might take. The guests' likely reaction will be somewhat defensive, which won't constructively contribute to acceptable levels of hospitality. For example, a guest is consumed by his feeling of irritation. He's been waiting for a long time to be served at a restaurant. None of the waiters seem to notice. Typically, a waiter that is receptive and consistently aware of the guest will anticipate and recognise his state of irritation immediately. Unfortunately, often this doesn't happen. Typically, the waiters are often mentally in 'operational mode', not noticing anything beyond their immediate task. Their unawareness creates a sort of tunnel vision which leaves their guests' needs unattended. Doubtless we've all have been subjected to such situations, where you feel invisible. This unawareness of service provision often isn't intentional; it's a general state of ignorance. It's obvious that the guest should be served as soon as possible; however, we should also consider other less obvious factors. Irritation and frustration is usually a cry for attention, and shouldn't be seen as an inconvenience to your service tasks. It is reasonable that an impatient guest is likely to voice their frustrations when their needs aren't being met. Complaints and frustrations should be seen as potential conduits to render recognition, appreciation and acceptance to another. This sounds rather dramatic; however, fundamentally this is the ultimate quest of service and hospitality: to alleviate discomfort and to host a secure and welcoming environment.

Ideally, first and foremost, we need to acknowledge the customer not solely as a financial beneficiary, but as a fellow human being. This is probably the most underrated of failures associated with poor customer approaches, and therefore also the most overlooked. The importance of basic recognition is crucial. What do we mean by 'recognition'? Various definitions are attributed to this concept. Nevertheless, for clarity on the topic I would like to concentrate on the augmented synonyms of 'identification', 'recollection' and 'appreciation'. It's quite possible to look, even stare, at someone without any recognition. We have all done that. That type of look is void of substance. It seems somewhat flat, one-dimensional and cursory. We see, but we don't have any affinity to what we are seeing. We are detached and indifferent. On the other hand, when one crosses paths with someone whom you recognise, you notice how both faces seemingly change with the process of recognition. Facial features tend to soften subsequent to the initial eye contact. Eyes that lock in this manner display qualities of recall and appreciation. This is customary for people who know each other and are positive about each other. Unfortunately with strangers this doesn't usually happen. We usually act indifferently.

We habitually observe others as separate from us. When not apathetic, and if we do in fact recognise them, this is generally recognising them as being different to us. Our minds tend to categorise everything. We have this impulsive need to place everything we receive through our senses within known categories, within our mind's historic thought structures. This frame of mind dictates the running course of our thoughts in all we perceive. That's why, as expressed in popular psychology, what we believe in becomes our reality. When we believe that we are different to others in any way, then we surely become exactly that. We become and remain different, for as long as such thoughts prevail in our minds. One could quite rightly ask, 'Am I supposed to not notice differences in other people?' Is this even possible?

A problem arises when we see 'difference' as a reference for who we seem to be. We look at something different; we attach a label to it, and then associate this label with other, related, mentally-ingrained labels. For example, when we see a designer-dressed stranger with an expressive frown, our minds might produce instantaneous associations of 'privilege', 'arrogant', or 'surly'. We might experience some reactive feelings of aversion, envy or smugness. This all occurs as though it's reality, as if we objectively see it as it is. We are convinced by whatever forms within our mind's eye. We believe all this, because this is what distinguishes us from others. It provides us with a clear identity. The ego therefore constantly strengthens this separateness, by compulsively portraying to everyone and everything tangible that we exist separate from others. The ego validates us. The ego sees all differences as a validation of itself; that it's unique and should assert itself as such. When threatened, the ego asserts itself to keep the identity it's created intact. If the ego does assert itself, it instantly feeds on the satisfaction of being different, better or even superior. Conversely, it may also feed on unsatisfied feelings of being worse off than others, inferior or weak.

We all know that initial impressions count. A lot of research has shown that first impressions are formed within the first seven seconds of contact. Before any word is spoken, the eyes signal intent. If for any reason the eyes aren't apparent, then demeanours and opposing energies are detected. The sensory points connect unconsciously within seconds. By the time this process becomes conscious, thoughts and associated labels have already been applied to the object. For example, my ego validates its made-up identity by instantly conjuring up a thought process that separates me from what I perceive. No matter what I perceive, be it a person's smile or a frown, I am not able to see it for what it is. I see a smile, and I think. I can't just see the smile without thinking. Perhaps I think: 'why is this person smiling?' I then try and read their minds. Perhaps I just assume that they are happy to see me. These various thought streams create the first impression, which involve body language, dress, posture and the various other communication signals. Most first impressions are already flawed by prejudice. This is absolutely natural. Our perceptive differences create psychological barriers that are unconsciously projected onto other people.

Are we then able to just look, without identifying totally with what our minds say about what we're looking at? Are we able to look without the compulsion to categorise or label? 'Yes' is my answer, and this is key to the hospitable mind. This exercise is simpler that one would expect. In effect we need to remove the analysing process from our minds. How are you able to observe anything without thought? Thought dissipates through being aware that you are thinking, or going to think. We need to develop the ability to become aware of thoughts. You already have this gift: it's part of your mental toolbox. When you meet a person, practice looking at them without thinking, and avoid labelling them as 'my scrounging colleague' or 'my emotional friend'. Mentally eradicate any descriptive adjectives. Focus on them, their entire being, without thought. If thought arises, become aware of it, and it magically goes away.

Why does this happen? By objectifying a thought or a feeling, a distance is created, and you instinctively know it's not part of you. It's not the true you. You are not your thoughts. If you are able to be aware of your thoughts, your thoughts must be separate from you. Then where does this awareness come from? Often it's described as the self, the non-ego entity which some call the soul, or the true and immortal consciousness. Without thought, the self becomes translucent, thereby able to connect directly with another entity. This is the most effective, most energetic way of truly connecting with people, animals, flora or any worldly thing. It's so fundamental that it's mostly overlooked by science. It's metaphysical, and can only be appreciated on a spiritual level.

By connecting without thought, we open ourselves to the 'being-ness' of others. It's an acceptance of what 'is' at the moment, without prejudice or expectations. Without thought, our being (self) shines through, and quite extraordinarily, it is usually reciprocated. I've personally have had some amazing shared experiences of this kind. Thinking back, it required very little effort; only the awareness of one's mindset is essential. Being aware that differences are a mental construct automatically shifts perception. You increasingly become aware of human 'sameness'. Therefore an empathetic shared dimension enters where once there was critical analysis. Your perception opens, the mind notices, but largely ignores the content of the thoughts. You instinctively know what you think isn't real. By knowing, you recognise and appreciate the other, as you do yourself. Aptly, in the bible, Mark (12:31) states, 'You must love your neighbour as yourself'. This means recognising that which is common among all human beings, their 'godliness', that appreciation of everyone having shared value. This is what love is all about, not just for humans, but for all entities that we encounter. It's recognising the similarity, the singular universal entity in all of us, which many call 'God'.

To achieve this type of awareness, all we should do is just be receptive. We could say that 'receptive' means accepting, acknowledging and eventually, listening. As we should recognise others, we also need to see ourselves through their eyes. This is a simultaneous process that really connects humans. This could turn out to be the single most important discovery you can make to cultivate your hospitable mind. All that this requires is a consistently open mind which focuses on the person, not on any 'issues'. Such an open mind recognises a fellow 'being' as just that, beyond form, dress or demeanour. For this to be accomplished you only have to accept others without mental divisions. That means making no categorisations, harbouring no predisposition or constructing any thought process. Accepting others, 'warts 'n all', is the magic key to hospitable nirvana. It's as simple as that.

It's unfortunate that as service staff, we are rather trained to act with technical consciousness, where effectiveness is measured by following correct procedures. Fulfilling tasks without the necessary attention given to the customer often is not enough. When we are subjected to unfavourable responses, often our knee-jerk reaction is to become defensive. We instantly attempt to justify our intents, feelings and actions. That's missing the point. We have totally missed the crucial recognition stage, the mutual validation of appreciation. After synergy is accomplished, a congruent base has been created for further action to take place. Only then can any positive result be reached with the ensuing thought-based issues. Thus, being attentive and aware of another's presence is a precursor to any effective communication.

'Do you want to be right, or do you want to be effective in your career?' My good friend and ex-boss Wouter Hensens used to ask our students, readying themselves for industrial placement. This typifies the pragmatic approach I've always preferred, currently more so for a different reason. Being right is satisfactory for the ego; however, it doesn't get you far in relationships. That part is quite intuitive. Considering the quote further, it illustrates that being right or wrong has nothing to do with being effective in work and in life. This is elementary, but it is not often considered. In the hospitable mind, 'effectiveness' is seen as true human connections that facilitate industry goals. Mindsets that harbour polarising thoughts divide us mentally, through differences, implying us being right and them being wrong. Polarising thoughts lead to similar emotions, and therefore disregard others' inner-beings entirely. It's the epitome of selfishness. Equally polarising emotions don't contribute remedies to a challenge, unless it's based on kindness and empathy.

Initially we shouldn't attempt to know or understand customers, nor the technicalities of a situation. Sure, there are various techniques for dealing with them and providing excellent service. There are endless literature sources to train these techniques into the skills you might need. Even if the customers' point of view is wrong, it's not going to be of any benefit to anyone to prove it so. However, what most people don't realise is that we need to connect on that basic level of appreciation before any effective service encounter can take place. With awareness, we notice that thoughts can become obstacles, labels could become ineffective in defining our perceptions, and prejudices should be disregarded.

## Transactional hospitality

'My, what a fine gentleman you are!' I was surprised at this comment, especially since it was totally uninvited. My being courteous had naturally prompted this lady in a supermarket to comment on my generosity. I had helped her by reaching for an item on the top shelf. My helpfulness was totally spontaneous, without any preconceived thought. However, I admit I was aware of my surroundings, feeling particularly positive toward the people around me and being mentally 'open to receiving an experience'. In other words, my mindset was conducive to my immediate surroundings, for no particular reason. The unsolicited compliment from this woman made me wonder: how do 'random acts of kindness' work? How come these acts feel so much better than those that are planned? What could I learn from this experience and how could I relate it to the cultivation of the hospitable mind?

We have all had events like these happen spontaneously, without premeditated input. That's significant. I generally regard myself as quite self-aware and I pride myself on being emotionally intelligent (except when I need to suffer fools!). I'm somewhat empathetic, although it's tempered by a high dose of meritocracy. I'm also persuasive when I need to be. However, empathy doesn't come naturally to me. What I'm getting at, is that all of us have tendencies towards different emotional, personality and character traits. So this is nothing abnormal (or so I hope). It all rather relative; we are all a little mad, however you might define and confer the appropriate labels. Considering mental health issues, in the past many diagnoses weren't identified because of the improper labels given to the severity of the conditions. As humans we are compulsive labellers, always trying to fit some strange, initially deformed, mental plug into our preconceived square mind-made holes. If it doesn't fit, we'll make it fit. A glorious thing the human mind is, forever attempting to subdue and adapt whatever we perceive to fit mental categories. On and on we go: submit, adapt, fit; submit, adapt and fit. Then when we perceive something we can't categorise, we get the closest related construct from our memory and pound it into submission to fit. What a miracle our brains are!

However, it's the process of adaptation that's most fascinating, as this is where wisdom culminates. There's a small, but not inconceivable 'space' between what we initially observe and the inevitable thought process that follows. Contrary to popular opinion, we are able to create a gap where we can regulate the stream of thoughts coming through our minds. Just as a physical reaction can be delayed, so mental activity can be slowed, even stopped. However, for this to happen, one needs the necessary awareness at that moment. This requires total attention to the present, so one can fully experience the immediate event. So how does this all relate to random acts of kindness, and the polarity of our thoughts and emotions?

Living your daily life fully in the present is creating the ideal conditions for random happenings of 'anything', which includes acts of kindness. Being present requires the mind to focus on what 'is', thereby pretty much eliminating thought. This has the effect of opening your mindset to receive, letting events happen without resistance. Opening your mind this way goes a long way in eradicating those thought-based polarities that we commonly experience. By definition, being present deletes past and future thoughts. Being fully present also effectively blocks any possible thought. Try thinking while you count from one to ten, or concentrate on your breathing. It stops thoughts dead. An added benefit is that being present and aware moderates extreme emotions. We effectively become 'even-tempered'. Thoughts facilitate mood swings, as they can linger and perpetuate other thoughts.

When we think, we become predisposed. When we are open and present, we function like a blank canvas, ready to receive whatever might be, a potential masterpiece. It becomes somewhat of an adventure. You have no idea what to expect, or what will happen. As an example, I typically prepare myself mentally before a networking event by consciously psyching myself up, either meditating or regulating my breathing, so as to manage my mindset. As an introvert, I do this in order to face others effectively. However, once I walk into the room I open my mind, I smile, and I absorb the whole environment with all of my senses. This way I'm restricting myself from revealing a specific demeanour, or a perceivable attitude, thereby tending to naturally draw people towards me. By expecting nothing, I'm able to remain in 'receiving' mode. Strangely, this is exactly where people respond to you effusively, and the simultaneous qualities of acceptance, appreciation and openness occur. Synergy develops.

The secret to fully listening to someone is not thinking what you are about to say, but focussing on understanding. As you maintain awareness, you can listen without thinking. With this 'awareness', don't just see it as focussing on an object or person, but as a receptiveness to your social surroundings, observing everything at once, without preconceived thought. When you're void of any thoughts, people respond because they instinctively feel the unconditional openness projected from within you. In turn, they naturally respond more intimately. Speech as a medium of communication then paradoxically takes a back seat to the awareness of this harmonious synergy. Communication is known to be so much more than just the words, gestures and other physical manifestations. Higher frequencies surpass the basic five human senses, and I believe there are even more metaphysical phenomena in communication waiting to be discovered. It's prudent to realise that what we cannot observe, isn't necessarily non-existent. My much more 'spiritually-in-touch' wife has informed me of this fact ad nauseam!

Reverting back to our discussion of 'awareness', when we become hospitable, we ideally warmly welcome and acknowledge our guests in a manner that avoids preconceptions about who they are. It should absolutely be inconsequential that they are paying for the privilege of our hospitality. It's also irrelevant whether they are rich, arrogant, or patronising. It should make no difference to us. This we can only achieve when we prevent interfering thoughts entirely. Luckily our minds are designed so that we are able to do this quite effectively. Most of us don't realise this. All it takes is an awareness of our current mindset, which means present observation of how thoughts flow in and out of our consciousness. Observation means just that, observing only, without judgement, so you experience a quiet confidence that thoughts are just thoughts, they aren't real. Once you start analysing thoughts, they become vicious circles of thought-streams that conjure up either the past or future. Past thoughts reflect beliefs, often unresolved histories and memorable life stories. Future thoughts reflect unfulfilled wishes, aspirations and hopes. None of them serve any real value, for you or the customer you might be serving. Nobody benefits by your thoughts. Even if you think 'happy' thoughts, realise that they're based on figments of your imagination. They're always associated with a previous experience, and therefore not real. They could serve you well, or could just as well be serving you loads of garbage. Just recognise thoughts for what they are; theoretical interpretations of what we empirically sense. A subjective filter is always present within our minds.

The 'transactional' relationship is central to all we accomplish in the commercial world. Every so often this also happens in our personal lives as well. The idea that 'one hand washes the other' is often mentioned when there's commercial gain involved. However necessary this might be in our lives, this also somewhat degrades authentic human connection. Being hospitable, whenever our connections with others become objectified, the practicality of the service process cuts out true connection. It inevitably results in a means to an end. We don't bother to become aware of the underlying presence of another person. Recognising that any preconceived thought could present itself at any time in our minds, requires us to train our mindset. When in the midst of trading or dealing with others, instinctively both parties know that there's some reciprocal motive lurking. Like the proverbial 'elephant in the room', is it something we need to address? Do you acknowledge or ignore it?

When we sell goods, consumption of those goods is usually fulfilled after the sale process has taken place. However, service assistance usually takes place before, during and after the goods are consumed. Thus service is consumed even before it is delivered, with an accumulation of many possible moments of truth. There are expectations, even before one buys. In hospitality, besides considering the goods (accommodation, food, facilities, etc.), the service processes can be quite intense and multi-dimensional, with a wide array of guests' needs to be fulfilled. So the reciprocal transactional motive is alive, well and kicking, with perceived 'value' that is to be delivered to the customers. As value is rather complex when applied to individual tastes and needs, their various expectations are difficult to determine. It's been an industry challenge how to effectively pin down the required delivery of standards in excellence. Ensuring that all hospitality staff are on the same page when delivering service is subject to massive quantities of training, some mission brainwashing, and copious amounts of objectives, sprinkled with a corporate vision. Many challenges obstruct this process, from high staff turnover to time and responsibility constraints. However, instead of looking to outward solutions, the fundamental place to work is from within each person involved.

The most memorable and highest level service delivered is absolutely reliant on the consistent recognition of the customer's being. When the server sees the customer as a means to an end, such as in procuring his tip, he will unconsciously project this. Such subliminal messages are highly susceptible to customers who are attentive to receiving 'value' driven signals, so that they can trust those who serve them in good faith. The perceived value invested into the service process needs to be justified. Any evasive, defensive or indifferent subliminal reaction from the server justifies and thus enhances the customer's opinion of 'poor service'. These reactions originate from the server's intentions, which are formed from internal beliefs and values that support habitual thought processes. When the server truly becomes focused on the customer as a person, seeing them without mentally constructing thoughts, the result is 'service' at the highest level. You effectively see what they see, though their eyes. You become them. You recognise yourself in them. This supersedes understanding of any given situation. It's as though you both unite. You become one. The mere fact of sharing presence in a moment of time creates the harmonious affinity for one another. This is the essence of the hospitable mind.

One could say that being hospitable is central to life. It seems to be part of the essence of our being, ingrained in our relationships. However, are we only being hospitable as a means to an end? Do we only do it to interact with those we deem worthy of our attention, in return receiving something of value? What motivates us to put in the effort? When we dislike someone, it seems as though the hospitable mindset becomes a chore that needs concerted effort. This perceived effort could cause our minds to banish personal attention and instead focus on predominantly destructive thoughts. We need to realise that perceptions originate at surface level, and often this is as far as we tend to look, with associated prejudiced thoughts and feelings. Looking beyond the surface to the being, with awareness and attention, is the answer. 'Liking' or 'not liking' is a preconceived notion, based on your personal social history, easily and often labelled onto others. With strangers this becomes more automatic, and erratic first impressions heavily set the subsequent trend of thoughts. Based on those irrational thoughts, we often make up our biased minds in a matter of seconds. However, since we need to function in an imperfect world, we need to be able to manage our own imperfect perceptions accordingly with ample awareness, but also remain aware that biased perceptions are part of the empirical reality we experience as humans. No matter how enlightened you might be on such matters, you will inevitably fail and fail again. Nevertheless, awareness is the most fundamental step to the unconditional hospitable mind.

## Finding that part of you called 'integrity'

In the past I tried to make sense of my chequered career and industry choices on many occasions, without much joy. My indecisiveness and lack of persistence became a comforting personal pattern of pursuit, where I didn't have to face the real consequences of responsibility, especially when the novelty of a new environment had worn off. Whenever I grew bored or frustrated, I found a convenient reason to emotionally and physically move off to somewhere more interesting. It became change for change's sake. Looking back and reflecting on my past jobs reveals an ugly demon, one of poor attitude and ignorance. However, unconsciously I accepted this passively most of the time, and did nothing further to prevent the inevitable decay of my self-confidence. Probably what bothered me most was that I wasn't bothered. Being young, free and seemingly invincible made me quite indifferent to the demands of life and work. This was the delusive situation I found myself in until I got involved in hospitality. After managing a family guesthouse, I wondered if I was even meant to pursue a career in the hospitality industry. Naturally I enjoyed the sunset cocktails with my guests, as this required me to be sociable and generous with the reciprocal funnelling of copious amounts of liquor. But however much fun these events might have been, facing guests with continued grace didn't come naturally to me. I had to consciously conjure up the required effort to make meaningful connections. Generally guests, especially those with a warped sense of superiority, annoyed me, which led me to become increasingly impatient serving others. Reflecting on these occurrences subsequently led me to ponder the workings of the hospitable mind. How do some individuals seem to have 'it', while many others, like me, find 'it' all rather elusive?

Many of us have been commercially bombarded by the 'secrets of success', where commercialised promoters promise the 'silver bullet' to everlasting happiness. With widespread exposure to social media, we see more and more articles showing us what we 'should be doing' within our daily lives that'll make us wealthy, happy and successful. We generally know about the value of effective communication; about the commitment needed to consistently perform and the motivational requirements to drive us to our goals. I've read hundreds of self-help, 'pop' and kitchen psychology books over the years, but I could never really realise and apply the often valid methods suggested. For example, following the advice of splitting up your habits into little teeny-weeny bite-sized accomplishments – yes, I get that! However, the practicalities of focussing your attention, intention, and proactive doing that brings those evasive accomplishments to realisation, is another logic altogether. Often unforeseen obstructive and distracting situations deter us from action. They seem to come from nowhere, curbing our enthusiasm. The resulting cycles of guilt and lack of self-confidence can rapidly spiral out of control in a negative way, affecting how we think, what we do and how we relate to others.

Taking these factors into consideration and consistently doing what we say, is imperative for others to take you seriously. That's not just being honest to others, but most importantly, to yourself. Being dishonest with yourself seems trivial. If only you know what you did or thought, so what? Does it really matter? Well it does become important if you are to remain aware of the consequences. If you are ignorant it won't matter until you are eventually forced by a consequential slap in the face with a wet fish, which results in a serious dose of self-hatred. The consequences of being disrespectful of your own integrity will not build needed confidence. It will not make you relate properly to other people. Similarly you will not bring any personal satisfaction to whatever you accomplish by being untruthful to yourself. 'Integrity' we identify as being fair, truthful, honest, sincere, and trustworthy, among other things. It's a highly abstract concept, thus quite difficult to digest meaningfully for most people. In general it also refers to 'wholeness', which means unifying yourself, and therefore also unifying yourself with others. This concept of unification is of utmost importance in the awareness of building your integrity, which involves breaking down barriers within yourself and the physical world. Unfortunately, the opposite human tendencies of 'separation' or 'identification' come more naturally to us.

We experience a lifelong history of labelling ourselves and others in order to make sense of our mental and physical environments. Intellectually it's absolutely necessary to be able to effectively function in this way; to categorise, and to establish a level of thinking that creates thought patterns. We use logic and rationalise abstract and tangible phenomena to form coherent arrangements within our own minds, as well as sustaining effective and logical communication with others. Thus to effectively cultivate the hospitable mind requires us to be vigilant in relation to the subtle balance of our rational mind and our recognition of others. This balance ensures that we remain consistently aware of the interplay between the virtues that underpin the wholeness of integrity.

I appreciate that this is easier said than done; however, the contents of this book should challenge you to ponder deeply about why you do what you do, and how to do what you are doing properly. When you are able to answer those questions with your whole being, you are able to unify your virtues, and integrity becomes integral. You will need to work from the inside out. It will not be effective to look around your environment for answers, or others' opinions of what you should do. No, not even from this book! Whatever you need to get to the answers, is already present within you. You just need to notice it. As it happens, integrity is also already present in you. You just need to relocate it, find it, accept it, and let it happen.

Anything you consistently think about or do (or don't do), eventually forms a habit. So it goes without saying that it's best to identify how to manage those habits most effectively. Managing your habits necessitates pre-empting your thoughts and feelings, observing their nature. Their nature is the conditioning of your mind, the consciousness you use to interpret your thoughts, and your surroundings. Habits are seen as somewhat 'unconscious', as they require less and less awareness to contemplate or perform, the more you use them. They are extremely useful tools to simplify your life and make it easier to directly respond to similar situations, such as brushing your teeth. Intuition (gut-feeling) can be seen as a further and higher level of abstraction; an unconscious thought evokes a 'feeling' related to previous, similar situations. In other words, we realise there's an interdependence of all things (and thoughts), and that all are directly derived from our mindset. The mindset is an accumulation of personal history, labels, paradigms, beliefs, opinions and prejudices, amongst other things. Nothing happens in isolation or in a vacuum. Every action has a reaction, which is followed by another action, and so on. The power and nature of our actions is firstly determined by our intentions. All changes in experience reflect an intention. An intention is not just desire; it also reflects human free will. When intentions are in conflict, and difficult choices need to be made, it fragments the mindset of the person. For example, when you need to choose between two promising career paths, you know they will bring different future results. These situations typically let you want to pursue both (this is known as getting your 'bread buttered on both sides'). This often moves you to 'straddle the fence' between both opportunities, becoming afraid to make the wrong choice.

However, being mindful, you shouldn't remain focussed on the opportunity not taken, thereby developing some useless regrets as result. You should rather focus on applying your unified self to the choice taken, fully accepting it and experiencing gratitude that you had the freedom to choose. Making seemingly big and important decisions displays fundamentally similar dynamics to making small, habitual decisions. For meaningful change, intentions are absolutely necessary. What we constantly think (and fret) about, we usually live out in some form or another. Thought patterns come out in an array of emotions, actions, responses or recurring thoughts. Our dispositions, aptitudes, and attitudes towards other people reflect our level of integrity. They are derived from our intentions. For example, when your disposition is one of prejudice, your intention comes across as judgemental. The essential trust necessary for the execution of an effective service will not be fulfilled. Your intentions stem from your connection with yourself as an integrative being, and therefore create the reality you experience with your customers or guests. This mostly happens unconsciously, until you become aware of it. Then you become 'mindful', thus observing the thoughts that pass through your mind. You are then able to identify the effect your actions and responses have on others. So how does all this transmit to the hospitable mindset? Integrity is closely related to one's clarity of intention, and thus a crucial element in all that encompasses hospitality.

## The necessary mindset

The hospitable mind is fundamental to encouraging others to enjoy themselves. Why is that? Making an appreciative and professional first impression as a host is an important prerequisite to creating the ideal hospitable environment. A hospitable demeanour relaxes the guests sufficiently, so they will also be receptive toward the host. This establishes the connective gateway enabling a mutual synergistic experience. Such positive demeanours lead to mutual participation, with accompanying trust. It follows that, with the right hospitable mindset, you will be able to increasingly transform customers' thought processes to enhance the service experience.

For people to thrive within a social setting, requires the facilitation of a collegial connection. Welcoming someone into your personal space requires some inquisitiveness from our side. We need to cultivate and experience our natural state of curiosity. Curiosity brings adventure in our daily humdrum existence. Like a child, we should become fascinated by all that touches our senses. Indulge some moments in others' beliefs, needs, aspirations and concerns. The American developmental psychologist Robert Kegan aptly states, 'The self-transforming mind can stand back from its own filter and look at it, not just through it. And why would it do so? Because the self-transforming mind both values and is wary about any one stance, analysis, or agenda.' To transform our minds, we need not only explore beyond our own minds, but also explore the workings within our minds, objectifying its prejudices.

Surrender to not focussing on yourself, and you will easily immerse yourself in listening, assisting, supporting, and empathising. This requires a certain vulnerability. Become aware of the person's presence in front of us, without being biased. It seems a contradiction in terms that unbiased thoughts are essentially a state of no-mind. The 'no-mind' describes a state of presence, where the current situation absorbs the mind-space completely, so that no predetermined thought interferes. Biased thoughts are derived from the remnants of social history, and are essentially thought-provoking. Unbiased thoughts are the opposite: being acceptant of the present condition. In a state of no-mind, you are receptive to facilitating effective response and action when needed, devoid of biased thoughts. For example, in difficult failed service situations you will have a better chance of effective remedial action by eliminating interfering thoughts. You might then even restore lost trust, and perhaps also manage to enhance loyalty.

The hospitable mind transcends commercially motivated thought processes. It even transcends the accompanying service considerations and requirements. It transcends individual beliefs, opinions, perceptions and prejudices. Yes, it even transcends thoughts. Within a no-mind state, the hospitable mind is thoughtless, but in a good way. Attention is projected onto another human being without the labelling of the other's perceived identity. By serving someone, you accept him or her as they are in that moment. There is nothing you need to add or take away, at that moment. You do not need to think, you only need to be attentive toward them. Recognising another in this way, says, 'I see you as the same as me'. I'm not your superior, nor am I your inferior. I already know you. I am here for you. I am you. I don't need to know anything more about you (however, you can share whatever you want with me, if you so wish). A similar mind-set is required to create friends and influence others.

Similarly, are you able to liaise and collaborate with colleagues effectively to succeed in the workplace? Are you able to reach out to strangers and get acquainted as equals? Working in teams and working closely with colleagues are integral to the industry, and having a similar no-mind approach to all those in our personal space is imperative. As for approaching strangers, I recognise that this could be an uncomfortable mindset for many; however, I would recommend it. Amazing experiences are to be gained by introducing yourself to strangers, and truly connecting. It teaches you much, besides increased self-confidence. Reflecting on this, I have come to realise that going into relationships without expectations, in a state of no-mind, has been a revelation in practice. The results have been encouraging indeed. This simple approach to really connecting with others is all that is fundamentally required from those who are serious in serving others.

As relationships with people are central to the hospitality industry, your main priority should be getting as much knowledge as possible in the expertise of service and determining human behaviour, right? No, not so. Every human is capable of providing the most exquisite hospitable experience. Although technical and operational skills are needed in industry to facilitate the transaction process efficiently and professionally, there remains a basic human tendency that is often overlooked. Attention given should be immediate and set within the present time. Attention is awareness of one's own mindset, as well as awareness of those who are working with you. I've been to an African mud hut in the middle of nowhere, where the hospitality provided from an uneducated man was on a par with the renowned Savoy Hotel in London. The absolute attentiveness of the host in providing for my every need was extraordinary. But it wasn't about what he did (technical prowess), but how it was delivered. I was acknowledged as a close friend (which I wasn't), and I was welcomed as a long lost brother (which I wasn't), and I was taken into confidence and trusted as a shared soul (which I felt I was). Totally unforgettable.

By exploring research articles of the required skills and competencies of successful hospitality professionals, one is entranced by the wide array of opinions that result. However, narrowing it all down to digestible conclusions, it is clear that a high percentage of industry leaders state the importance of soft skills: emotional intelligence, personality, and transferable skills. Ironically, much of what is taught in universities and higher education institutions doesn't adequately cover these fields of knowledge. The primary message here is that you don't need to experience a fancy hotel school or university to learn that magic formula. The source is already within you. You just need to discover it for yourself. Nevertheless, it would be most beneficial to experience a truly conducive professional environment for inspiration. I went to the fancy hotel school, and got a similarly fancy education. Personally, it didn't give me any superior advantage when it came to the technicalities of my service delivery. In fact, it somewhat drew me away from being attentive to others, as I became much more analytical in my approach.

Customers would pick up on this, seeing me as often as aloof and condescending. In my mind I was doing all the right things. I was going through the correct service processes with scalpel-sharp precision, knowing my product features by heart, displaying my superior knowledge and savvy business acumen. Yes, I impressed some, and intimidated others; however, I could never really claim that I had an extraordinary guest experience. Suffice to say, they had no idea of my brilliance, of course! So was that education money well spent? Obviously I'm being rather facetious about my education. It did provide me with great opportunities further down the line, especially in academia. My point is that what really counts in the industry, isn't what you know, but how you apply your natural abilities to providing service to others, be it customers or colleagues. It's that easy. Like most things in life that are truly effective, simplicity is widely underestimated. When you consider this industry, it's not primarily about honing your intellectual abilities. It's about harnessing your natural abilities to identify yourself with and within others. This manifests as truly caring about others, being compassionate, empathetic, and thereby being hospitable.

## We serve, but are not servants

Expectations are ever-present in humans. It's a natural condition of the thought-filled mind. Indeed it's an inevitable condition of our customers' value-derived minds too. Expectations arise with the need to achieve and control future outcomes. Anticipating the customer's expectations requires a mind that is attuned to their needs. It requires us to be alert in acquiring the means to satisfy their needs. Likewise it requires us to care enough, to respect, and to empathise with their current situation. When we come across as influential, likeable, and trusted in the presence of others, we really become receptive to their needs. We recognise this especially when we are acutely aware of our own mindset, and able to eliminate intrusive thoughts. By becoming aware, we consciously enhance our attention and focus on the person's presence. Modifying our social skills to consistently achieve this special connection then becomes effortless. With practice this happens unconsciously. It becomes a by-product of true recognition. It might seem as though some people possess this trait naturally. They are apparently able to turn this quality on like a light switch whenever needed, without obvious effort. Such role models include superstar professionals of the hospitality world, the health carers, the charity workers, and those alleviating human suffering.

Over the years, I have found that several of my hospitality students demonstrated these 'loftier social skills' within their work placements. Subsequently they have achieved much industry success, seemingly because of this specific mindset. On the other hand, some have also managed spectacular blunders because of their evident lack of these abilities. All of our lives, we are socially predetermined to being in service to others, and thus responsible for providing common benefit to all. Our social effectiveness is reliant on this mindset, which in turn determines our actions and reactions to others. It is often necessary for us to reflect upon and re-evaluate progress on our inner 'charm school', thereby sharpening our social skills. We should reassess the type of influence we have on the people we face daily. Many spiritualists and behavioural scientists have substantiated the karmic consequences of our behaviours, so there's much to contemplate if you are serious about improving your social performance.

Being a slave to prejudice and opinion has proven to be an obstacle to effective social communication. Yet being open-minded and accepting has the opposite effect, and brings acceptance in return. An analogy could be the young child's curiosity about life, where all seems fresh, unlabelled, and innocent. In many ways the ignorance of the child is characterised as thoughtlessness, as they have an unconditional acceptance of all worldly things. They are often fascinated by, and curious about, strange things they have not experienced yet. For example, a toddler would approach many potentially dangerous objects with attention and anticipating joy. For them there isn't any attached historical context. There's no fear. It typifies the proverb that 'ignorance is bliss'. It's intriguing that we can't quite fathom the obvious: that our thoughts (and fears) often get in the way of us being truly attentive.

Being attentive to the presence of something, or someone, isn't the same as being attentive to what we are thinking. The sources of attentiveness are different. During verbal conversation, we usually think about first impressions, what we should say, reflect on what was said, and then think about what to say next. If fact, much of what's said to us quite often goes astray, because our thoughts don't allow us to really listen. As we grow older, we increasingly associate with our history, our environment, and our life stories. We soak up our societal influences, which mentally condition us. Consequently, we become more individualised, with self-serving motives and self-seeking rewards. Constantly ruminating on these past thought processes, beliefs and experiences has the effect of manifesting similar present and future realities. We act according to our thoughts, which are our past stories recurring in the present. As result of this psycho-social conditioning, we detect other humans as different to us. We are determining and defining our own existence according to our perception of the material world. We perceive ourselves as separate from the world and the rest of humanity. 'My world' is a historically driven mental construct where I separate myself from others' worlds. There's no such thing as 'my world' or 'my life', as you don't own either. It also assumes that 'you' and the 'world' or 'life' are separate from each other, which you are not. You are part of the totality of particles present in the universe, and you will always be so.

However, reasoning with a logical mind frequently doesn't gain much credibility for my 'one world' viewpoint. Successful industry people are commonly endorsed by their competitiveness in furiously playing the 'me versus them' field, so well represented within their careers and ambitions. It ultimately becomes the 'survival of the fittest' to claim the ultimate prize. This dominant and competitive attitude can easily divide opinion, build walls, create prejudice, and vindicate differences between beings. However, when these competitive attributes are controlled and balanced with the correct context and personal intent, then they will appropriately benefit all concerned. Extreme types of competitiveness have no viable claim to benefit the hospitable mind, as they will often prevent true connection between people. They weaken collaboration and enable a lack of empathy. To be able to function socially at your highest level in hospitality requires an awareness of these potentially divisive attitudes. Predominantly this means looking within one's self, and only thereafter seeking the truth from your guests or colleagues. You are never able to totally control what others might think of you; however, you are able to deal with yourself. You should become increasingly aware of observing your own thoughts. When the moment of truth occurs, do you still carry on thinking, or do you pay full attention to your guest, with no intruding thoughts?

Unfortunately, any thoughts are fundamentally flawed when we initially connect with others. They might be good, bad or indifferent thoughts; however, they will still be highly subjective. In other words, there's no real benefit in trying to determine the 'real truth' in mentally analysing somebody. Thoughts only cloud our real need to connect. Putting thought aside when we are facing another person is key. It puts us in the present moment. It opens our minds and makes us receptive to truly connect with their being. This is the first step in the attempt to understand another. Many people have no idea how to pause the incessant stream of thinking they experience. Many never realise that thoughts can be stopped for some periods of time. Many also think that stopping thought will have no real benefit. Buddhist monks and meditation practitioners across the ages have shown the real benefits resulting from no-mind rituals. So how do you stop thought? It is quite simple really, and I'll regularly refer to it during the course of this book.

Focussed attention on the subject or object is an obvious method; not looking at it by labelling or analysing it, not even naming it, but just looking at it. The idea is not to stare, of course! However, you should look not superficially, with your eyes, but deeper, with your being. You should look at the essence of what you're looking at. If it's a person, then become attentive to the being inside that person. Look beyond the material form in front of you. Look through their eyes, beyond the physical. Try and see yourself in them. You might experience this awareness as peripheral vision and other sensory sensations. It probably seems weird for most people I speak to, but it works. It may surprise you how consistently it works when you are able to deeply connect with total strangers in this way. Another method often deployed is concentrating on your breathing, being aware how your breath flows in and out, just before your social encounter. This creates the required space in your mind. Keep in mind that inevitably thoughts will occur within a short period of time thereafter (perhaps in seconds), to fulfil service processes completely and effectively. Nevertheless the brief moments of attentive acknowledgement are precious and should be savoured, as they pave the way to a superior hospitable experience. During subsequent verbal pauses in the ensuing conversations, you may continue to practice no-mind at intervals, to deeply reconnect again at suitable times.

Being truly hospitable is a humbling experience indeed, and therefore large egos aren't welcome. Whether you function as a dishwasher, a manager or the 'big cheese', to serve remains the most important role throughout your career. You will effectively serve all, from guests to stakeholders, even your own employees. However, serving doesn't mean you are second class, or inferior, to anybody else. In fact, servers throughout history have shaped the world for the better, as they have lived their lives beyond their own interests, caring about others, thereby creating a better life for all.

## Being hospitable is natural

Fundamentally, 'being ourselves' typically eliminates fear. We normally achieve this by being comfortable in familiar surroundings and within a well-known social structure. This becomes obvious when we entertain our best friends and family. Usually, we do not have to pretend or to be cautious in conversing with them. Unpleasant social surprises are minimised by a feeling of familiarity, where interactions needed between familiar acquaintances are less reliant on our thought processes. We mentally and physically relax (unless we have a strained relationship with them). Our social skills aren't as vigilantly obvious, and conscious thought often becomes of secondary importance. This creates that essential space for connection. When we refer to 'space', we mean a space for emotional and thought 'chill time'. We just mentally pause for a relaxing, thoughtless break in the stream of life. Accordingly deeper connections happen when such a space is created, where our thoughts don't require defined expression. The space created should not prompt you to fill it up with something. When you are at ease with the space (which could consist of silence or no-mind), you don't feel the need to fill it with thoughts, distractions or outside stimulation. Most people feel compelled to fill up every moment with something, as if being in a state of 'busyness' is constantly required. There's this socially-infused drive that life needs to consist of every satisfactory sensory experience possible. It's almost as if any space that appears should be eradicated, that it represents some form of 'living waste'. When we enter a space with another human, miraculously both beings become susceptible to mentally opening up to each other. The potential feelings of apprehension (or fear) are therefore replaced by mutual acceptance. Our sense of independence is transformed into shared care. Awareness of these qualities does much to cultivate the hospitable mind.

Being hospitable to people we care about is easy, for we have existing positive reciprocal emotions that reinforce our actions. With less effort, we feel as though the interaction we go through will result in worthwhile mutual experiences. We naturally believe these efforts will be reciprocated at some stage, once again demonstrating how well we are able to return to our unguarded and trustful origins, when we were an innocent child. Often, we don't even expect an encouraging reaction from those close to us. We get that warm fuzzy feeling that we have contributed to someone's happiness, without any expectations that it should be returned. It's so easy to forget that essentially everyone anticipates a feeling of being welcomed and acknowledged, without apprehension. However, the mind constantly accumulates thoughts that are seeking, questioning, and reasoning. This often prevents us from opening ourselves to others. The mind innately reverts to thoughts, unconsciously processing endless streams of self-reflection. Some research publications state that at least 50,000 thoughts cross our mind daily; equal to 35 per minute. In view of this, we undoubtedly seem to be over-consumed by internal thoughts. How often do we take the time to focus on our immediate surroundings? How often are we able to give ample attention to others, undistracted by our own thoughts? Now combine this with the constant disruptive streams of media we are forced to face, and it's no wonder we are prone to mental health problems.

You need adequate space within your mindset to empower yourself to manage the streams of outside and inside 'noise'. Unless you move to an isolated environment, like a Buddhist monastery, there's no escaping this often intrusive noise. You might not always be able to control the outside noise, yet it's very much up to you to do something useful about your inner noise. This means creating an area or dimension of 'space' within your mind. This space is a prerequisite to paying unbiased attention to an object, person, or environment you find yourself in at a given moment. Most interestingly, once we combine our myriad of feelings with incessant streams of self-absorbing thoughts, the mind becomes cluttered with three-dimensional combinations of mental commotion. This does nothing for us when we are required to give quality attention to others. Once we are engrossed in our own minds or electronic devices, the presence of others often becomes an irritating inconvenience to us. We are often oblivious to their feelings, needs or disposition. In fact we are oblivious to everything. We've seen the often calamitous consequences:

people gawking at their mobile phones, walking into lampposts or worse, into oncoming traffic. However, when we allow the required space to focus on others, our prejudices and emotions dissipate into the background, thereby allowing that connection. Although initially difficult to comprehend, this required psychological space can be thought of as similar to the role of silence within music. Think of the space that occurs as the snippets of silence between the audible notes in music. The music would not be identified as a melody, if it wasn't for those strategically spaced silences. It would just sound like the most dreadful clamour. Also reflect on the massive space (more than 99%) that surrounds the nucleus of atoms within the hardest of metals. Similarly, we are gifted with the opportunity to create mental space whenever it is needed in our lives. Buddhist Master Osho says, 'The deeper your watchfulness becomes, the deeper your awareness becomes, and gaps start arising, intervals. One thought goes and another has not come, and there is a gap. One cloud has passed, another is coming and there is a gap. In those gaps, for the first time you will have glimpses of no-mind, you will have the taste of no-mind.' Within the hospitable mind, we endeavour to cultivate this no-mind, so that we're able to liberate our awareness. This enables us to create the space necessary to focus on whatever is presented in front of us.

Ralf Waldo Emerson remarked, 'The invariable mark of wisdom is to see the miraculous in the common.' Are we naturally susceptible to small miracles? We need to be receptive, attentive and aware to facilitate this ability. This is nature's gift to us. As humans, we are already adequately equipped to be able to experience small miracles in life. However, to experience these miracles in our social and hospitable environments, we need to create space in our minds to make way for awareness of this gift. Advertisers use this concept in their designs, and call it 'white space', where simple messages don't need to be extravagantly illustrated to get requisite responses. Once you make space in the continual stream of thoughts within your mind, you provide that space for the common to become exceptional. We should realise that the uncluttered mind is a prerequisite to effective communication. Although we have the common notion that we can 'multi-task', we cannot effectively 'multi-think'. We cannot consciously process more than one thought at a time.

Sometimes, the more we are trained in technical skills, filled with theoretical mental constructs, the less we are in touch with our fundamental awareness skills. This is the case unless we create space. What we learn, believe and understand about life and work, colours our perceptions, how we process our thoughts. Whether they are true or valuable is beside the point, as they still provide obstacles to clearing thoughts from our minds. In other words, they keep us from truly connecting with our deeper selves and the world. As the learner driver struggles with the techniques of driving by consciously performing perplexing ambidextrous movements, nervously attempting 360 degree vision, accompanied by erratic signalling, they experience simultaneous streams of mental anguish. With many hours of practice, the learner's driving increasingly becomes unconscious; he then can become aware of the pleasurable sensations and the feeling of freedom when driving. Correspondingly, we only gain confidence and dissipate fear when space in the mind is created, whenever we become aware of our thoughts passing through our minds.

Stopping mental noise is often difficult, and not really necessary. We only need to become aware of the thoughts as an outsider, looking into our minds. By objectifying our thoughts, we create a space for observation. From some distance, we witness the mental stream as a filmstrip passing by. With added curiosity we can stay distantly amused at the content, therefore not taking it seriously and recognising it for what it is – historical narratives of our experiences. Seeing the workings of your mind in this way, makes any thoughts and associated feelings benign, and therefore they gently fade away. We subsequently become more mentally naïve, whereas the spaces that appear progressively supply us with the necessary attention to truly connect to others. The naïve mind is open, fresh, and creative. The naïve mind is fearless and shows natural courage and self-confidence. Famously it is stated in the Bible, 'the meek shall inherit the earth', which implies that the naïve mind will triumph over the egotistical. True confidence is revealed in candour and being forthright with others. It has a quality of brave vulnerability. Conversely, arrogance is fear-based, and begs the need for self-justification.

Guests require worthwhile attention. This is profoundly good for business too. Any professional in this industry recognises that attentiveness is one of the key ingredients to high-level hospitality experiences. We do guests a disservice when we cannot give them the full attention they have paid for, and psychologically crave. Being hospitable is seemingly natural, as all of us have successfully entertained others. Why is it then such a persistent challenge for the industry? Intuitively, one knows when your mindset is attuned to being hospitable. But as we have seen, it's much easier with people we actually like. However, to function at optimal level as a professional, one needs to perform at a higher level consistently, and that's where the desired mindset is critical. To converse properly with peers, customers and stakeholders you should sustain your awareness, allowing mental spaces for deeper bonds to flourish. If you do, a sense of sharing, unity, and kindred spirit will come across noticeably. These bonds enhance the cultivation of the hospitable mind.

## The commercial mindset

We all realise that our social standards of acceptance are often different toward strangers than friends. In industry, we normally compensate for our underlying insecurities by applying a friendly persona. When we serve, this involves making a conscious decision to perform hospitable activities for commercial gain. And here we notice another apparent paradox. As previously discussed, the ideal hospitable mind relies on total acceptance and openness in serving others without prejudice, but on the other hand, commercial hospitality necessitates the requisition of economic value. These circumstances seem to be contradictory in terms of the objectives. We might argue that commercial gain somewhat dissolves much of the sincere purposes of hospitality. Nevertheless, to be effective in the industry, one must reconcile different priorities: your personal and career growth with company performance objectives.

The primary company objective is financial sustainability. This is usually non-negotiable. However, we shouldn't regard this fact as a threat to being truly hospitable. These seeming opposites of the winning equation could become an exciting personal challenge. The company is usually very clear on priorities: excellent service and maximising profits. As this is an inevitable situation for the company, this shouldn't pose too much of a personal struggle. Logically, what the company pursues doesn't have to reflect directly on your personal values. Collectively following capitalistic ideals for others doesn't necessarily align with achieving your own personal ideals. Personal ideals are more likely to be related to ambitions, achievement, personal growth and the (illusory) search for happiness. Note that most of these ideals mentioned are not prioritised by the companies that employ you. When working in industry, payment for service can feel somewhat like prostituting yourself. We often serve to the best of our ability, but there's always some customer that reminds you that you are effectively just a 'means to an end'. These customers may say that because you are being paid, they can disregard your humanity, show little respect, and treat you like a second-class citizen. This is to be your spiritual journey as a hospitality practitioner. Personally it requires you to focus your attention beyond trading off two opposites, which would be deep connectivity as opposed to commercial gain. Personally, your growth is determined by creating your own beneficial career path. Being drawn toward pragmatic ideals is great; however, that doesn't serve your personal growth. You can go through the motions of a daily job, or you can pursue the pinnacle of providing sincere service to the world. For this, you will need to sustain awareness of your own prejudices, and avoid labelling customers according to their means. Only when we attend to others' immediate presence, despite the underlying commercial conventions, does mutual acceptance and virtuousness arise.

When the customer displays anger at unrealised commercial value, maintaining your attention to remain open, aware and present will undoubtedly remedy the situation. Similar to how a lone dog's barking quickly tires when it is not reciprocated, the agitated customer soon calms down when faced with a caring and attentive server who recognises them beyond their façade or financial means. What's the potential outcome? The troubled situation, without mutually fuelled emotions and the mutual acceptance of the other as fellow humans, diminishes.

The hospitable mind not only yields a caring outlook toward others, but also prompts us to develop a personal purpose in serving others' needs. Consciously or unconsciously, developing some form of a 'caring' purpose is basic in cultivating a hospitable mind. To be hospitable requires care, and to care makes you hospitable, so as to warmly receive others. This epitomises the classic riddle of the 'chicken or egg' relationship: which comes first? As in the riddle, it's very much irrelevant, as both are psychologically present within one's traits, and they need to develop in tandem. However, the awareness of care needs to be practised to become part of us, with thoughts and intention, in attitude, and manifested in action. As we progress in our hospitable mindset, we consequently become attuned to the needs of others, and thus we care more intimately. This ultimately leads us to approach the commercialised environment of industry with a higher level of purpose and awareness of what really needs to be accomplished. The theme of caring is explored in further detail in chapter four.

When we enter the commercial world of work, we often become conflicted because of the pursuit of profits, and the essential nature of our industry. These apparently opposed standards of the industry need to be well understood in the context of our mindset, so as to function, and progress, effectively as managers. To become responsible and credible industry managers, it is imperative to be profit-orientated in your business approach. Your leadership performance is partly judged on the financial results you produce, which require costs to be minimised and revenues to be maximised, without undue detriment to guests and other stakeholders. However, this is often where many managers come unstuck, as they seek shortcuts to profit, setting unscrupulous paths that are often unethical and devious, so as to ensure positive short-term outcomes.

Every managerial decision has some ethical element inherent to its execution, as the outcomes always affect the people involved in some shape or form. Often, in the pursuit of short-term goals such as profits, long-term considerations are conveniently left hanging. These long-term outcomes could be environmental impacts, growth, staff wellbeing, or loss of the company's market share. Most often it would be a combination of these, as poor management has been shown to affect companies adversely as a whole. Commercially, prolonged disastrous leadership has shown to have had catastrophic effects on communities, employees and their families. There's a high demand for well-balanced and responsible leadership in the industry; however, many young recruits are initially disillusioned by the vague and ineffective supervisory skills of their superiors. New recruits are often unsure of their given responsibilities, provided with limited support and having their expected results vaguely outlined. They invariably leave the industry earlier than expected, pursuing a path less stressful, better waged, and with improved prospects. These transient staff conditions in the industry lead to high turnover in jobs, which increases costs in recruiting, training, and settling them into fully functional and productive employees. Traditionally this is the most costly labour issue in the hospitality industry, and thus a common denominator that all companies must overcome. However, it's been shown that the best working environments also keep the best talents for longer, thus they become good indicators for best practice in management and industry-standard leadership.

Capitalism needn't clash with being hospitable. When one approaches your hospitable skillset with honesty, openness and non-judgement, it becomes a sure means of fulfilment, and therefore an end in itself. Capitalism becomes merely a means to an end. Doing that one thing you can do well, with dedicated attention, is all the effort you need to gain long-term positive results. Take that as a lifetime guarantee. Giving the necessary positive attention to the present moment leads inevitably to a positive outcome in the future. Besides this being particularly evident in hospitality, it's prevalent in all walks of life. Provide attention to the present moment, whatever your situation might be, with focus and commitment. Accept what the moment delivers no matter what. This mindset has the magical ability to transform your life and career for the better. It leads to joy in whatever you do, and doing this consistently ensures contentment.

## Pursuing means, not rewards

Knowing that the audience for this book will be curious in expanding their understanding of how the mind works, it would be prudent to explore the role performance and ambition plays in the context of the industry. Monitoring and keeping abreast of improvements in terms of performance indicators are certainly useful tools for our personal development. Typically you will receive feedback on your job performance, with appraisals once or more times per annum. These are rather formal, and their effectiveness can be doubtful, depending on how they are conducted, and the extent of constructive feedback given. To increase performance it's necessary to reflect on both the adverse and conducive situations experienced. Employees typically become defensive when confronted with undue criticism that challenges their established performance levels. Initial reactions may trigger fear, anger, denial or other rationalised emotions. When caught up in these situations one naturally feels strongly about justifying one's behaviour or actions. We often feel as though our identities are being threatened when confronted by our weaknesses.

Our minds contain certain thoughts about ourselves which help to create our identities; this is also based on others' previous perceptions and social justifications. When we receive criticism of our efforts, we feel as though we are being attacked directly in terms of whom we perceive we 'are', and subsequently, our worth. This is because we falsely perceive our 'self' as the accumulation of our historic stories, associated labels and others' perceived ideas of who we are. This is the fabricated content of our thoughts, and to us, it seems logical and very real. It feels as though is it indeed 'us'. Yet, the critical remarks are essentially aimed at a fictitious persona, from the fictional mindset of someone else. There's absolutely no direct or divine source or right to judge anyone like this. It's important to realise that this muddled path of discourse cannot be construed as necessarily true. Therefore, whenever we reflect on and are reflected upon by others, we shouldn't judge ourselves according to their expectations.

Unfortunately, when we are young and impressionable, conflicting opinions often become all-consuming. In the mix, also throw in magnitudes of emotions and you see immense misperceptions wreaking havoc on our already volatile confidence levels. Once again, working from the inside out, we need to reflect on our own responsibilities and performance objectives, without identifying with our labelled outcomes ('success', 'fail', 'loser', 'ambitious', 'under-achiever', etc.). When freeing ourselves from labels, we get into constructive dialogue in our minds. We are able to depersonalise our disappointments by diverting them away from our identities, and we are able to remain empathetic to ourselves. This is crucial to retaining and sustaining our self-respect, especially after challenging periods of personal turmoil.

Many will state that a tough 'talking to' yourself is needed to invoke the required discipline to perform at your best level. By all means, be frank with yourself, be honest and open. Just don't be swayed by the torrent of emotionally laden misleading thoughts that frequent troubled mindsets. They are there to strengthen the ego, to build fear and further insecurities. This mindset seduces us to play the victim, to lay blame elsewhere, anywhere opportune. Indeed, it takes a certain humbling attitude to admit fault, defeat, or wrongdoing. However, being truly sorry, empathetic and forgiving yourself holds the immensely liberating promise of revitalising a dire situation. It's so much easier if you know where the thoughts actually originate from. It frees you from guilt, disposes of useless historical thought, resentment and other distractions.

We tend to see our ultimate reward in life as some form of material success. This is understandable, as much of our success conditioning comes from the media's stereotypical glitzy glamour. Success is largely about the anticipation created by society's consumer indoctrinations and its effect on our senses throughout our lives. While we generally accept that success is an individual matter, we are intentionally and subliminally nurtured by what society regards as 'success'. What does success mean to you as you dedicate yourself to the industry? What do you see as the ultimate reward? What will you feel like when this 'ideal' state of being is reached? These are all questions we struggle to pin down as we freshly approach our careers and, if we're fortunate, sorting it out quickly is best for clarity of purpose.

By popular opinion, we are told to get single-minded about a specific ambition, to focus on setting appropriate goals clearly, and not to stray from the path. Logically this makes sense, as the shortest path is planned, straight and focused. It's the path that we feel is individual to us, predetermined, strategic and narrow. Our parents, peers and closest confidants all encourage us to apply ourselves with discipline, stoically devoting ourselves to our purpose. This in turn creates emotional certainty for them, eases their worries, and makes you a stable, investable subject to soothe their consciences. Inevitably it will, in turn, make them feel good about themselves that they have had a positive effect on your, but also their, success. However noble these well-meaning gestures seem to be, people close to us are often incapable of unconditionally accepting us or our decisions. Quite often they fear for our sake and anticipate often imaginary disastrous consequences. This is mostly well-intended concern for our well-being. However, there's a fine line between providing valued guidance on request, and stifling our personal growth.

To manage your own path, it's best to take all advice with circumspection, giving context to when and where it originates from. Solicited or not, you always learn from every situation, be it good or bad. It's crucial to assess and reflect on the value gained from the information received. Maintain a thoughtful and emotional distance from others' influence. Conversely, a kneejerk negative reaction is never of much benefit. It will only hurt others' feelings and damage a relationship. We need to realise that we don't have to react or comply to other's views if it is not necessary. We are in control of our own thoughts and emotions, and having no reaction is within that sphere of control as well. Taking any advice on board is totally your choice. Understandably, once you follow someone's advice you forfeit some of the responsibility for your own behaviour and the actions associated with the advice given. You never entirely own what you've decided, thus you are somewhat absolved from the responsibly that comes from its consequences. Accordingly you have more reason to blame something or someone else when things don't work out, when you give up or when you fail. A great part of the feeling that you are evolving toward your ambitions is to know that you followed your own decisions, and have taken effective ownership of your life and career situations. That doesn't mean you should endure the path on your own. Everyone needs others to accomplish valuable things. However, taking ownership focusses us on the responsibilities and risk that have been bestowed upon us. Whenever others provide much of the surety, it diminishes the satisfaction of personal performance somewhat. It's much like winning the lottery, where little effort equates to huge rewards. The rewards should be sweet; however, the element of pure luck, without fortitude, involved is often perceived as a hindering factor to lasting satisfaction. Dr Susan David, a psychology academic from Harvard University, quite accurately stated, 'discomfort is the price of admission to a meaningful life'. In order for us to feel as though we have sufficient purpose, we need to feel that our efforts justify the outcomes, or else it becomes a somewhat hollow victory.

## CHAPTER 2

# Being responsive: are you aligned or are you resistant?

*"Question: What is your sector looking for in young graduates?*
*Answer: A positive attitude first, last and always,*
*followed closely by an open mindset willing to embrace change,*
*as well as a sincere desire to continue to learn*
*and grow as an individual."*

**Bruce Harkness,**
**Senior Vice-President, Human Resources of Wyndham Asia Pacific**

## Mapping achievements

Being responsive is a key attribute to service delivery, and also for consistent high-level performance. Being psychologically and physically responsive, you are able to give important and urgent matters the required attention. This entails active commitment, discipline, motivation, and awareness. It certainly also suggests that you have a clear sense of purpose. Many contemporary psychologists mention the search for purpose that drives us to do great things. There are strong relationships between the concepts of 'purpose', 'aims', 'goals', and 'vision'. Theoretically the concepts are all different, but they are all necessary key drivers for personal motivation, forming a progressive plan towards our ideas of what we want to accomplish. The ideas of 'purpose' and 'sense of worth' are also very personal to our own mindsets. They enrich our evolving feelings of self-confidence. So, how are you able to control yourself and your circumstances to reach your goals, therefore feeling you have a purpose?

Rationally, goal-setting is a useful and necessary exercise to achieve determined outcomes. These outcomes, goals or objectives should preferably be written down in detail, in order to make it as tangible as possible for the mind to absorb. Thoughts are often fleeting, racing through our minds like scared rabbits. When ideas are written down, they have a better chance of surviving prolonged attention, especially if they are continuously and consciously referred to. There are many valuable sources to refer to on how to do goal-setting in detail. Keeping to the theme of the book, I shall only concentrate on the mindset required. What you are effectively doing in this exercise, is creating a 'map' of where you would like to go and end up, in work and in life. In my opinion they are one and the same, as enjoyable work will by definition become an integral part of your enjoyable life. Therefore it will cease to be 'work'. Once you reach a state of enjoyment in the work that you do, it won't be work anymore, it just becomes life. Yes, you will still play a distinct role as a professional; however, it will be one of many others.

We can only set goals within our own context. We cannot realistically set goals for anyone else. Goals should constantly aim at improving the individual on his own terms, at his own pace and with his own specific desired outcomes. Realise that everybody enters the proverbial rat race at different points in their life. There's no common finishing line, and no mutually-agreed achievement scale. The playing field is yours only, and it's as vast as you want it to be. However, you have to stick to your own race to make it valued, to sustain the necessary motivation for your own idea of success. Success cannot be based on someone else's idea of accomplishment. Living in an instant gratification, speed-hungry and attention-grabbing society, the common mindset frequently pursues the 'least effort' to an end, the quickest path to apparent success. Quite often this success portrays the publicly glorified, materialistic, and leisurely lifestyle of the glam society. Identifying with these one-dimensional views of accomplishment invariably leads to inferiority complexes, mired with feelings of low self-worth and resentment.

Ambitious goals dictate a lifestyle change, where your resources need to be aligned with your desired outcomes. To be accomplished at something or gain expertise, some research results indicated that an excess of 10,000 hours need to be devoted to the specific discipline. 'Something's gotta give' means some opportunity cost needs to be considered, where time and effort is needed in major quantities. 'Opportunity cost' is when you devote your effort and time to an opportunity, yet realising and appreciating that other opportunities inevitably can't be attended to, and are therefore lost. Managing your available time is crucial. Ambitious goals typically are challenging to follow, and therefore a clear and purposeful mindset is key. This requires the individual to form appropriate habits in the long term. According to the experts, steady combinations of small but challenging steps pave the way to more challenging performances. Gradual progression is the preferred method likely to be sustained by motivation. Therefore it's a more desirable route to follow for self-fulfilment and reaching aspirations.

To commit ourselves to a goal, it needs to be worthy. How do we assess the worthiness of goals? The most intuitive way is to find the big picture to validate what we are trying to accomplish. Contemplating this holistically might seem rather abstract to the uninitiated. What are the things that make you 'tick', get you out of bed, blow your hair back, push your boat, or generally make your life worthwhile? Establishing a life purpose is no easy task. Often we feel as though we've been put on earth by default, for no particular reason, seemingly by random cosmic arrangement. We are given an environment we haven't had any conscious choice in, born from unknown parents, unsolicited and 'forced' into a society not of our own making. However, we are expected to perform tricks within this weird circus to keep it all going like clockwork and entertain the crowds, otherwise we will be ostracised as abnormal, labelled as anti-social or delinquent. Yes, you are dealt a pack of cards that seems random.

However, with the appropriate mindset, reality, as perceived by you, can be shaped, modified and created according to the thoughts you entertain. It forms your habits, as well as the values and beliefs you hold. However, a life purpose could very easily remain one of life's unsolved mysteries, and indeed for many it does until they die. I would recommend that you face this mystery head-on. Don't wait until it becomes apparent on your deathbed! Consciously circumventing a philosophical essay on 'purpose', I'll attempt to contribute more to your understanding by keeping it simple. Simple things are often the most effective. I assume you are reading this book because of your interest in hospitality. I also assume your interest in service, care and human behaviour are somewhat aligned with your fundamental values. Notwithstanding the various ambitions that you may have, these values will normally stay fairly steady amidst the changing aspirations that ebb and flow throughout life. You will need to establish which of these values mentioned are the most representative of your mental outlook. Contemplate the things that matter most to you.

Write down the things that are most important to you, and create a statement (or two...) from their meanings and interpretations. Note that these statements shouldn't specify desired future outcomes. You should already have these abilities as part of your mindset. In other words, these values aren't to be acquired. They should be 'realised' from within, and come naturally to awareness. The subconscious should be made conscious. Articulating these statements is modelling your purpose, which therefore becomes a personal vision statement. To illustrate this, I've included my own career vision and purpose with a quote from Nelson Henderson: 'The true meaning of life is to plant trees, under whose shade you do not expect to sit". This quote describes what my values represent in one concise sentence. To me it represents the values of education, duty of care, my service ethic, and my understanding of altruism.

On the other hand, a professional mission statement is different to a purpose, as it merely indicates a path toward your purpose. In other words a mission shows how you can reach your purpose. A mission is a statement (or two) of intent linked to key objectives. The mission can then further be broken up into separate detailed objectives, with linked strategies to be actioned. Once again to illustrate my own, I've narrated it as: 'to educate, mentor, and facilitate students, graduates and employees to fully engage with their work and to fulfil their career ambitions in the Hospitality industry'. Working from general to specifics keeps your holistic purpose in your mind's eye, thereby preserving your career purpose in whatever you plan. Conversely, it also stimulates your mindset when you define your small and achievable goals, by expressing how you are planning to achieve them within the wider scope of your purpose. Once these goals are both written down and internalised, let them rest and refer to them periodically when needed. Key in the process of planning is to stay in the moment. If your focus is solely on achieving, or on the outcome, you will seek the path of least resistance. You are more likely to copy others, act insincerely, and forfeit your higher values to gain quick results. Most likely you will lose the joy of development and self-discovery, effectively avoiding a fulfilling career path as a means to an end.

Take action to achieve what you can now, instead of hoping and wishing that the elusive motivation, ability and effort will turn up later. We often have valid excuses for not doing what we set out to do: being lazy, being sick, or rearranging your closet. Eventually, if you persist in finding excuses, it becomes a habit. Sometimes we are under the illusion that we only have ourselves to answer to, that it's okay, and that means we get off easy. Not so, as we can undermine our self-worth and self-respect quite harmfully, without outside help. With prolonged denial, it becomes exceedingly difficult to be honest with ourselves on these matters. We are most often the worst person to answer to. Our minds often rationalise our lack of self-motivation in a way that we don't have to explain to ourselves. Nobody (hopefully) notices or reprimands us. When not being scrutinised, responsibility and accountability isn't brought into the mind's equation. However unconsciously, our minds will suffer with this as it regurgitates rationalised thoughts. The mind sustains these stories as you convince yourself that it is true. With habit, we often deny ourselves the chance to even reflect on it. 'Being honest with yourself' ceases to exist. If we do become aware, the 'penny will drop' (we become aware), and we'll find that these mental constructs are mere delusions.

If you haven't been the most hospitable person but you wish you were, ask yourself: 'What are my favourite excuses for not putting in the consistent effort required?' Reflect on the validity of the excuses and the habits that lead to them. 'How can I counteract these excuses?' Reflect on how you can take charge and re-script negative thought patterns. Then integrate these with your goal plan. Yes, you do need to plan, set goals and contemplate strategic moves; however, recognise the immediate mindset's thought processes and emotions for what they are, either constructive or destructive. Being aware in the moment, means that you are able to separate yourself from those thoughts and emotions. By becoming aware of their fleeting nature, you are immune to their influence and potential destructiveness. Unaffected, you are able to focus on the required task with the fullest attention. Recognise that an excessive ego becomes a block to awareness. It says, 'I'm better than this', 'I shouldn't be here' or 'I deserve this'. Transcending your troubled ego-driven thoughts renews motivation, continues commitment and sustains awareness.

Pursuing a goal often becomes an end in itself. The human mind commonly rationalises the quickest, easiest route to desired outcomes. Delayed gratification isn't fashionable, partly because of our post-war commercialised society. We are conditioned to consume, buy on credit, seek attention, and glorify material gain. The 'end in mind' becomes all defining, and frustrated people often seek the shortest possible route to the next 'fix'. It boosts our self-image, and feeds the insatiable ego. Instead of focusing on the current moment, the mind thwarts the present by relying on the reassurance of past thoughts. We all wait for that illusive 'ship to come in'. By focussing on the moment, the resulting awareness moderates your intrusive thoughts to the point of them being irrelevant to your state of confidence. Your confidence levels remain steady as long as your awareness of presence persists. When a goal is achieved without the required effort or merit, it usually smacks of a hollow victory that doesn't satisfy or give real, lasting pleasure. These emotional outcomes aren't always consciously understood. However at the time the rewards seem sweet. Inevitably it eventually permeates into a cycle of personal discouragement, further rationalisation, diminished motivation and ultimately, unhappiness.

Contrariwise, when you achieve successes in line with your purpose, it moves beyond the outer confirmation of your self-confidence, as your thoughts and actions have evolved from within your values. Success becomes less important as a label to identify yourself by. It will come as no surprise that you will have no need to be recognised for accomplishments. You may even find that your own self-worth will not be dependent on any results, success or achievement. This begs the question: with no external need for identity and self-worth, why do we still pursue achievement?

The best way to view this is by contemplating our role as it plays out on the stage of life. This is an apt analogy, as we tend to determine the character roles we pick, as well as how we act according to prescribed scripts, within the limited show time on the stage set. How we act and play out these roles has an effect on our performance. It leads to personal accomplishments and ultimately, also contributes to the overall success of the show. For the show to be successful, you need to be successful irrespective of others' outcomes. As such, if your values are not aligned to collaborating with the rest of the human race, there's something very wrong in how you define your specific role, and therefore, your purpose. The stage set illustrates just how dependent we are on each other, and how crucial every living entity is to the favourable outcome of the whole. It's logical then to notice that all values need to be based on serving the whole. How is this achieved? By simply working from the inside out. After loving yourself, you can start loving your neighbour, as the Bible states in the second commandment. Achievement then is supposed to be pursued for the sake of the all, to 'honour and love', as marriage vows so aptly describe. Common achievement, an enhancement of the whole, is 'success' redefined.

Inevitably, we need the support of others to achieve. Some people make us feel grand about ourselves, such as close family and friends. However, they don't often contribute much in evolving our social skills. Surrounding yourself with agreeable people will often lead to lower levels of self-assessment, with complacent feelings of self-efficacy. You effectively remain warm, fuzzy and habitually cosy within your own delusions of ability. Reflecting on the effects of your preconceived thoughts is often a consequence of personal strife. It often requires difficult situations to bring home valuable messages. These cause us to reflect on our attitudes and our levels of emotional intelligence. When you dig deep enough, you will realise that the most difficult situations frequently demand a heightened understanding. In turn this can lead to an intensified awareness.

The hospitality 'hotshots' (or high achievers) I've known often displayed the capacity to reflect upon their motivation during challenging incidents. They consistently explored their behaviour through self-analysis. They understood that their thought processes were subject to a specific context. Knowing the effect of their habitual reactions as they impacted on others stirred mental awareness out of its dormancy. Thus achievers developed a heightened awareness of their own emotional and thought processes. By understanding how these mind processes manifest, one also understands how to best control them.

## Enthusiasm through awareness

People respond to enthusiasm. It's contagious. Most human resource practitioners simply describe this mindset as a 'positive attitude'. It is often said that one hires staff for the right attitude; knowledge and experience can be gained on the job, whereas attitude often can't. It's seen as a trait that can't necessarily be cultivated by the accumulation of experience. However, being aware of how our attitudes influence situations is imperative. We often cannot remove ourselves from our reactions. We become those reactions, with associated thoughts and feelings intertwined. Awareness of the fact that we are able to control or even distance ourselves from our reactions is rather difficult. For as we think, we often unconsciously act.

Few of us contemplate the possibility of the vast resources beyond the thinking mind. For consistency, I have referred to it as awareness. Awareness is when we separate ourselves from our conscious thoughts, which initially seems improbable. This part of us is only able to present itself when we objectify our stream of thoughts as a separate entity. Passively perceiving our thoughts as they momentarily arise in our minds is the fundamental requisite of awareness. This means that we should observe whatever comes into our minds without judgement or additional commentary. Attention is different. It's the conscious diminishing of various thoughts toward a concentrated few, thereby intently focussing on something or someone in present time. For a sustained positive attitude, both awareness and attention are required. The interplay between awareness and attention creates the ideal conditions for a positive attitude to flourish. Consistently practising these mental states will eventually focus your mindset on stable, value-based beliefs. These beliefs then actively contribute to lasting habits and strong discipline.

When communicating with others, truly positive convictions cannot be faked. When you act and speak from deeply ingrained convictions, you come across as authentic. Enthusiasm naturally comes from within, without much motivational effort. Whenever you act out a conviction without belief, you will soon be caught out, or most probably you will lose interest. Having strong convictions can work well for you, or equally well against you, depending on your motives and intentions. Convictions accompanied by strong enthusiasm often cloud our perceptions, for better or worse. This combination can progress individuals' behaviour to greater performance or likewise lead them to increased closed-mindedness. This can lead to a higher state of ignorance. By showing conviction in any situation, you often forget that your influence only extends as far as you are able to have an effect on others' perceptions. Often, we need to remind ourselves that we're not able to 'control' the thoughts of others. They will think whatever they want to think, and perceive life's situations through the context of their own historical perceptions. The best you can hope for is that the positive impact of your efforts may, in turn, positively influence others' thoughts and actions. The simplest, most effective and consistent method to achieve this is to become aware of the natural alignment between yourself and the others you interact with. Nothing said or shown will speak as loudly as someone's full attention and awareness of the person they are attending to. This shows true commitment and conviction. This results into enthusiasm, which is contagious and infused with energy.

We often aren't aware of the natural alignment between people. Paradoxically, we pursue some unnatural ways to maintain personal relationships. We habitually feel we should demonstrate our individuality to relate to others. From a young age, we are socially conditioned to see ourselves as proud individualistic beings, protecting our fragile identities in all we do. We pride ourselves in being unique, exhibiting our own choices of lifestyle, developing our specific mannerisms, insisting on standing out from the crowd. We become somewhat obsessed with ourselves. Additionally, with the promise of money, you seem to be fortunate enough to purchase your preferred identity, lifestyle and anything else that matters to you most. However, we normally never realise that our identities are inherently more delicate than we realise. They depend heavily on others' verification of what is deemed virtuous, which is ultimately flawed by social consensus. Please note that I don't propose the abolition of social norms or material wealth; not at all! What I'm suggesting here is that it should be seen in context. Those worldly props are needed to successfully act out your role on this life stage, to star in the show with conviction and enthusiasm. Realise that props are just props, not part of, or an indication of, your true identity. Yet it's an important part of the temporary role you play throughout your life.

Returning to the nativity paradox, when babies or toddlers socialise they are accepting of all they come in contact with. They don't seem to notice any separateness, as the concept hasn't been implanted in them yet. Many primitive societies, too, show similar collective tendencies; many generations have close-knit families and strong community bonds. However in modern societies, we differentiate ourselves according to categories, imaginary borders and labels that are completely thought-based. Once we appreciate that our thoughts limit the way we see others, we understand and become aware of our similarity to others. We notice our mindset limitations less, especially when we question our own ideas in the way we perceive ourselves and others. Equally, we then also notice other peoples' mindset limitations more, regard them with more empathy, and view all humans in a similar positive light, despite their shortcomings. Whenever we approach a social activity that requires our fullest attention, the deciding factors that determine the outcome in the situation, typically, are our attitude and level of expectations. Both sustain our motivational levels.

So what should we realistically expect from others? Beyond the limited level of influence we have on others, not much else can be expected. In fact, not expecting anything at all often opens the door to positive experiences. Keeping an open mind means accepting situations and persons with total confidence. You consciously accept that they cannot be under your control. Nor would you desire to have them under your control, as responsibility for their behaviour will ultimately revert to you. What people do, or don't do, think or expect of you is actually none of your business. Attempting to read someone else's mind is pointless. If you happen to get it right, it comes across as patronising. If you get it wrong, you voluntarily succumb to a potential dispute. Not having any expectations results in a liberating sense of personal freedom even when the experiences aren't ideal. Developing this mindset, we can sustain our enthusiasm and focus on what we are able to contribute to the present situation, rather than relying on factors outside our control.

## Pointless comparisons

Observing highly talented hospitality professionals at work can be quite inspiring. I vividly remember my childhood travel to a fancy hotel in Austria, and a particular impression a concierge made on me. He seemed to know everything. I was in awe, not just of his breadth of knowledge, but the charming way he dispensed it. At the same time I found it demoralising. How could I ever be that good, that smart, and even that handsome? What effect do comparisons have on you? Do they perhaps make you feel incompetent or inferior? Unintentionally we feel the need to compare. It's as though we need to reassure ourselves that we exist, and that we matter. We desperately need to convince ourselves that we're a separate and valued human being.

We learn from benchmarking ourselves, our attributes and qualities to others. Our role-models often inspire us to achieve more, provide us with increased motivation, and lessons in progress. They are valuable indeed, as their experiences help guide us, like signposts. We identify with their life's context and how it relates to ours. Comparisons allow us to learn from these signs; however, we need to realise every path taken is unique. We can never really understand someone else's situation fully. 'Putting yourself in someone else's shoes' merely does lip service to the fact: a great and noble thought indeed. However, 'treating someone like you would like to be treated', is somewhat more realistic, as you are the only one who knows your story best.

Comparisons as a useful tool can enhance our understanding of our social inefficiencies somewhat, depending on how they are utilised. However, comparisons hardly ever have constructive outcomes for our self-identity. Comparisons are always relative and bounded by context. Even though we are unique individuals, we are all essentially the same. We are socialised to be unique, told and encouraged to be different, and yet, without the labels, physical differences and words, we are all the same. Our individual self-identity is made up. So expertly made up, in fact, that it actually seems as though it's all we have. Our identity is conceptually constructed to be 'comparable', so that we can create our own disparate life contexts. Our limitations become apparent as we're hot-wired by communal norms to benchmark ourselves to others' attributes, possessions, or talents. There are always those who are smarter, richer, uglier or worse-off than us. Nevertheless, individual performances are essential in fulfilling life's aspirations of achievement. Therefore we feel our self-identity is subject to how we are perceived, and dependent on what we accomplish. Here the ego has an important function. If managed correctly, it drives our thoughts and emotions to perform actions, especially during those primeval 'fight or flight' reactions where anger and fear were once so essential for survival. Nevertheless, our egos also feed on comparisons, as we tend to feel good when we are seen as superior, and less so when not affirmed as such. Fragile or inflated egos are easily threatened, and need to be continuously supported to survive. If we don't favourably compare to others, our sense of self-identity diminishes. Our motivation suffers. However, it's necessary to clarify that self-identity isn't the 'self', meaning me. Self-identity is the ego personified. Self-identity is the conceptualised mind, where the ego strives via thoughts to relax or perform, to create pain or pleasure, to conquer or destroy. These are all essential tasks in managing life properly. On the other hand, the essential 'self' doesn't diminish others to improve oneself. The 'self' doesn't separate itself from others by comparison. It has no conscious thought process. However, it underlies and observes all thought. It's manifested awareness.

## Sustained habits

Discipline is important, as it creates consistency. Motivation feeds consistency, and in turn, consistency does much to sustain motivation. The discipline of a well-structured personal agenda gives us an effective canvas on which to paint a system of consistencies with detailed goal-setting. However, as planning is clarifying a design path, the next step is moving forward with consistent action. Such action is dependent on sustained motivation, and a disciplined approach to behaviour. Research shows that habits are essential to save us from mental effort. Any routine functions or repetitive thoughts are psychologically encoded to become habits, always travelling the same neural paths. This natural human and animal instinct frees up mental capacity to pursue other more vital thought processes.

Motivation can be sustained by habits. It's like a muscle that needs consistent strengthening, but easily gets fatigued when used too much. Habitual behaviour eases the path for motivation to occur, especially when it's constructively planned for increased performance. Habits basically consist of triggers, routines and rewards. The idea is to create or modify our habits in the ideal way to achieve our goals. That means analysing how our habits have been formed and what impact they have had in our lives. Triggers are just that: an initial urge that moves us toward a certain thought, emotion or action. Once we identify the nature of the specific triggers that set our habits in motion, we can modify them, or create better substitutes. This analysis requires one to reflect upon the origins, circumstances, and impact of the triggers. Then the routine of the habit can be redesigned or modified according to what needs to be achieved. A simple example would be to form a habit of smiling at every customer who walks through the front door, no matter who it might be. A consistent and effective trigger needs to be found or designed, which could be as simple as a ringing doorbell, or taking a deep breath. It could be more elaborate, like the first words of a greeting procedure, or stepping out from behind a desk. Thereafter it needs to be consciously practiced until it becomes unconscious, just like the inexperienced driver needs to practise until actions become automatic.

Habit relies on routine. Routine is the combination of tactics followed to reach the desired outcomes. Initially these tactics should require enough effort to feel as though you have progressed and achieved a 'small win' as reward. However, too much effort often ensures a high chance of failure. It isn't recommended, as it will discourage your continuation of the routine. Non-challenging routines will not work either, as continuing performance and motivation will suffer. Easy challenges also provide little value in terms of reward. Through consistently small but challenging wins, momentum will develop motivational levels and the habitual patterns will eventually fully embed within our mindset to form a stable habit. When trying to change an existing habit, the rewards should provide a comparable type of satisfaction as previously gained to be consistently effective. Thus after the routine, a suitable reward needs to be clearly acknowledged. As logical and obvious as this might seem, often rewards are not well defined, and therefore not well recognised when achieved. Analysing the value of rewards is quite fascinating. Defining rewards is not as straightforward as one would expect. Often we associate reward with something we 'get', whereas it's mostly something about how we 'feel' when we get it. Often, the feeling of achievement is the 'high' we feel, not the fact that we got extra money as a bonus. The sweet treat we reward ourselves after we successfully complete a fitness session is not so much about the substance of the treat, but more about the way it makes us feel when we eat it. After such a physically demanding session, it's often the indulgence in something 'naughty but nice' that entices us. Ultimately it's the experience, not the ownership, which stimulates us most as a reward. The realisation of this mindset can have significant resulting impacts when mapping our goals and expected rewards.

## The confidence edifice

It is well documented by research that increased confidence is conducive and positively correlated to motivation. Self-confidence, in relation to efficacy, affects the way you feel you have performed, and how satisfied you feel you are with the choices you made. It is important to realise that the context of your beliefs is dependent on the perception of your ability. Any powerful feeling of confidence is based on past happenings and interpreted scenarios, where you have had the desired positive outcomes. It's important to know that your level of confidence doesn't necessarily reflect what has transpired, but how it has appeared to you at the time, with your subsequent thoughts of it. One has to realise that these thoughts and beliefs are fleeting. They originate inside the mind and are subject to coloured perceptions of what we believe is 'true' from our history and social interactions. None of this is real in fundamental terms. Only by questioning the workings of our minds, do we become aware of this liberating fact. The management of our minds as a necessary life-tool should be a conscious daily action. By managing, I mean objectifying our thought processes, recognising the archetypal human tendency to take our emotional and thought reactions seriously. We should move beyond our mind's stereotypical and predictable processing. Objectifying your thoughts moves you to a quiet space of awareness. This awareness comes from noticing your emotions and thoughts arising, not avoiding or denying their existence. Also don't attempt to fight against it, or revel in it, or attach your identity to it. Instead of an immediate reaction, just notice as it passes through your consciousness. Once you've acknowledged the thoughts, move your superfluous attention to your present situation. Understandably, we cannot ignore our human tendencies, and we shouldn't. However, a certain level of healthy confidence is necessary to get our worldly ambitions realised. Confidence is highly dependent on a state of mind that honours the present moment with immediate attention. Sustained confidence necessitates subtle but synergetic interchanges between our mindset, awareness and immediate external factors.

Four routes to self-efficacy are illustrated here to build self-confidence. The first of these are mastery experiences, which refer to situations where you feel you have succeeded in the past. You need to build these success references continuously to gain confidence, but not so that you become smug. Often in this case, one develops a closed mindset to what you know and are comfortable with. Likewise, one can get a false sense of security (a self-enhanced mindset of the self) that could manifest as complacency and arrogance. This is contrary to remaining open to learning, to experiencing new and more adventurous avenues of expression. Your daily life is habitually made up of mundane events, which are an accumulation of many small successes and failures. Opening yourself up to fully experience daily goings-on brings you clarity about your self-efficacy. Constant progress with small successes leads the way to larger goals, and more determined habits.

Secondly, you receive indirect experiences by seeing people who are similar to you succeed. Others' successes have an influence on your perception of your abilities and motivation. As mentioned before, any comparisons need to be holistically assessed. As such, 'role-models' can be a powerful motivation or demotivation. Do you see you and your model's inherent qualities in a similar light? What can you learn from them? Placing them on the proverbial mental 'pedestal', when they have achieved worldly success, could be harming our motivational and confidence levels. It's prudent to realise that we can learn from other; however, we should never compare ourselves with them.

A detrimental human tendency is to compare life situations. This has no real benefit to us, as it's essentially a false resemblance to the truth. Nobody can be compared to anyone else. We often judge others' achievements, and see them either as conducive or detrimental to our own motivational levels. We need to be reminded that all humans are essentially equal, and should be perceived with similar regard, irrespective of worldly importance or prominence. We have all judged and been judged before in our lives. These incidents are not always perceived as being fair.

Sometimes credible individuals have the capacity to disappoint and infuriate others with out-of-character behaviour. All sane minds invoke some form of psychotic behaviour occasionally. To some relative degree, we are all stark-raving mad. Some of these traits are somewhat normalised within our personal mental constitution. Only by expert observation can these traits become recognised for what they seem to be, and labelled accordingly. It is sensible to develop our own 'fresh eyes' in observing our own use of mental traits without bias. With valuable insight we can gain some control over our fickle mental states and emotional intelligence. To progress, we should always remain inquisitive as to how we and our social environments could be managed with more finesse. Learn from all people's behaviour, good, bad or indifferent. However, real challenges, such as disappointment, sorrow and strife, shift us furthest towards awareness.

Disappointment means that you had some expectations that weren't met. As mentioned before, expectations are hugely overvalued as a social tool. They do not add value to your well-being. Expectations require a situation or someone's input to make us feel in a certain way. This input can come either from others or ourselves. When we remain open and attentive to any form of input, regardless of our expectations, then we are able to connect fully with any situation or person. An example would be facing a complaint from a guest. When we initially hear about it, we mentally pre-empt the argument before we even face the guest. This places us in 'defensive mode' where our preconceived ideas have already manifested a scenario of conflict. Our predisposition is ready to receive the expected input that justifies our thoughts. Even if the matter isn't as severe as expected when faced with the guest, our expectant disposition could easily further intensify our defensive attitude.

Having no expectations, one doesn't regard the nature or context of the input as important. You realise you should not take things at face value. We see the bigger picture, beyond the obvious. We don't distinguish anyone by their apparent labels or roles. We also realise we are diverse from our mindset origins, and that we develop uniquely from separate psycho-social paradigms. However, besides our fleeting human-made thoughts and aging physical bodies, we are essentially the same. When we truly look at others in essence, we realise that we are looking in the mirror. This recognition will eventually surface as kindness. It's a basic, but inherent trait of every person: to appreciate others as fellow human beings.

Social persuasion is a third route to self-efficacy; hearing from others that you are capable, you feel that you are receiving the necessary validation for your efforts. We do tend to rely too much on others' encouragement that we are 'in control'. I say 'in control', as in essence, it's a fickle illusion we all devour. Control is seductive, and high doses often lead to all-consuming ideas of power. Power essentially forces our mindset into 'separateness' in terms of our ability. We position ourselves as mentally superior to others. Social validation of our actions originates from this delusion, originally from others' thought processes projected upon us. Everyone is subject to similar mental delusions in some way, no matter what level of power you think you possess. Not surprisingly, the saying that 'a rich man's integrity is measured by the way he treats a waiter' is quite apt to illustrate the responsible use of power. Actually, power dissolves totally when we relate to others with awareness.

Not that there's anything wrong with using power responsibly; in fact it's an effective self-drive energy for our career performance and promises the pursuit of excellence. However, one needs to keep in mind that power remains conceptual, thus not true nor absolute. Everyone that seems powerful eventually turns to ashes. Yet this is where our egos rationalise other's reactions as true reflections of our abilities. The more we receive approval, the more we feel we are confident, so we then pursue more confidence-building actions. Often, higher levels of power are conducive to heightened thoughts and emotions. Subsequent positive and negative events perpetuate amplified reactions, so as to justify the power awarded. This illustrates how misrepresented power often corrupts minds, and how so-called leaders turn into evil dictators.

These mindsets originate out of delusions of grandeur, where such persons see themselves as superior, different and higher in stature than their fellow humans. Labelling themselves inappropriately superior sustains their self-derived identities and inflated egos. In time they will inevitably feel compelled to label others within their environment suitably inferior. These labels may range from expletives to terms of endearment, clearly identifying their friends and foes. These delusive labels become so attached to their various mindsets that they become fact, and therefore become ultimately 'true'. This, in turn, develops into a long-standing belief, which further enhances their ignorance and arrogance. On the other hand, the preferred mindset acquires awareness to see past labels, recognising all beings beyond their preconceived identities and outward semblances.

Truly aware people will not pressure you to do anything you wouldn't want to do, as they know that only you should take responsibility for your actions. By giving others the freedom to make or change their decisions, opinions or actions, you show respect and awareness for their being. Do people who communicate with you stress you in any way? Do they truly recognise you, not for what you can do for them, but for whom you essentially are? I'd say this happens occasionally, and instinctively you know it when you experience it. The compulsion to assist or guide others in life is ever-seductive. Advice is great when asked for; however, when not, it could revert to one-sided condescending views. We cannot coerce people into saying good things about us, but we can always choose how we feel about them. Our emotional states and resulting reactions when something is said to us are of great importance in enhancing our confidence. Taking into consideration that others will encourage or discourage our actions with love and compassion, it should be seen as a generous act of caring. However, sometimes it might seem like self-enhancing prejudices. With awareness we are able to see it for what it is, and practice remaining strong in any situation.

Fourth, and therefore the final route to self-efficacy, is regulating your emotional status. Effective regulation is when you are able to stay positive and manage stress. This suggests that you have control of your emotions, which is often easier said than done. Emotions are sometimes misleadingly presumed to happen before thought, which implies that they can be triggered by mere physical events, such as an attack from a bear. This is not the case; for fear to appear as a split-second thought in our minds, with the subsequent reaction in our bodies, we need to attach a label to the object from preceding thought processes. Without these socialised and object-attached labels, we will not feel this fear. This phenomenon is quite apparent in research into babies and young toddlers, before such psycho-social influences are internalised.

However, our emotional outlook is a fantastic tool to enhance our confidence and therefore also our motivational levels. For example, we can use it to boost our feelings of joy or gratitude in contributing to others. We can use anger to express our dissatisfaction at having our expectations unfulfilled, and demanding satisfaction. As humans we tend to express our emotions based on our perceived life situations and our expectations. Expectations originate from our thoughts, and are directly related to the past and future connotations we ascribe to events. How these events play out in our perceptions leave either mental traces of pain or pleasure. Contrary to popular opinion, we actually have control of these traces. By concentrating on recycling the pain or pleasure that has passed through our minds in the past, we can modify them accordingly. We can also essentially eliminate these painful traces altogether by focussing on the present, realising that all such traces were subject to mind-made origins, not reality. By realising that we are not our thoughts, we also realise that we are not our emotions. This is, once again, truly liberating.

When we distance ourselves from, and therefore question, our thoughts and associated labelling, we see our emotions as a virtuous tool that can be used to enhance our confidence when needed. We should never deny our emotions, however good, bad or indifferent. Denying them won't eliminate them. It will just temporarily push them into the dark recesses of the mind, ready to surface at the first adverse opportunity. Just noticing your human emotions with acceptance brings much-needed space between perceptive thoughts and instant reactions. We all know that knee-jerk reactions are never beneficial for volatile social situations. However, we all need emotional states to feel deeply and appreciate life's worth. Similarly we need productive thoughts and emotions to pursue and achieve our life's ambitions.

## Thoughtful successes

The more success we experience, the more likely it is we will enjoy success in the future. Often, what worked for us in the past becomes part of our future. Is this at all surprising, as our thoughts have conditioned the world for us? So yes, to some extent the usual kitchen psychology is correct here: what you think determinates what you do, and who you ultimately become. Moderation of the mind is necessary to curb the excessive ego. Practically, this involves a reflective awareness of your quality of thoughts. Objectifying your intentions and idea-formation will create the necessary mental distance to regulate the ego and its inevitable consequential reactions. Once again, 'objectifying' here means observing thoughts and situations unfolding in the present, and thus attending to it with the fullest attention as it happens.

However, this is only one part of the equation. The other part refers to an essential time dimension. Our thoughts are time-dependent, as they originate from our historical stories. Thinking is not reality, it is preconceived notions, including who you are, what you are, why you are doing what you are doing, and how you think you are doing it. We believe the labels we are given, and we believe what we see and think about everything. Since we were born, we were told to believe, but what is there to believe apart from our thoughts and convictions? Should we believe our perceived and conceptualised world? It is all made up. However this is not a problem for us as we, once again, can use this to our advantage. We just need to keep in mind that just as 'successes' are good, so too are 'failures'. They are relative, and can essentially be seen as the same conduit to progress. They can be seen as a means to an end. They are not results; they are the process, the journey. They are the required state to get you where 'you would want to be'. Note that I do not mention where you 'want to end up', for there is no real state of ending up. Where you would want to be is where you are right here, right now. A future or past mindset isn't helpful. This now is all that you have, and is infinitely more 'real'. Many philosophers would argue that what we presently experience isn't real either. However intellectually you would like to argue about this, the fact is that the present time is all you have. If you would like to be better at something in the future, that's fine. You can only consistently work on it, and give attention to it in the now. There's only now. And once you have thought about it, it's gone. So when you think about your previous successes, you are reliving the past, and that can give you some required encouragement, through reliving your past experiences. However, thinking about it doesn't mean doing it, although it does support the action to be taken. Thus thought precedes action.

Success is a mind-made state, and therefore another conceptual label. What does this label indicate to you? It cannot be argued that it's a very personal choice, seen as completely individualistic. We conjure up all kinds of thoughts about what it means to us. Is there a true indication of success? The mainstream media bombard us with popularised notions of success. Irrefutably this contributes to controversial societal standards, showcasing fashionable tendencies to achievement. This is the world we live in: we breathe it, we consume it, and we socialise it ad nauseam. The concept 'achieve success' itself, implies a separate condition to be reached. It presupposes us to be in a state of 'not having', and needing to get to it. When we eventually arrive, we will be labelled 'successful'. When we don't arrive at this mind-made destination, we are deemed to have 'failed'. How crazy is that?

Even if we achieve our own definition of success, does that mean we have now fulfilled our dreams and have therefore become happy? The short answer is 'no', as future concepts are based on past thoughts, which are based on our ego requirements for satisfaction. Having something, like 'success', is an achievement celebrated by the ego, to make the self feel good about itself. Once again it's a productive tool, but it shouldn't be seen as real or lasting. We may lose ourselves within the illusion of the self, becoming somewhat arrogant about our increased successes in the world. Often, many seemingly successful people turn out to be sad, troubled and unappreciative despite their apparent good fortune. Many suffer from depression. Their productive mindset has obviously done well for them; however, it would seem as though their inner-being still suffers. The mass illusion of their identity could come as a rude awakening. Perhaps they weren't the person everybody expected them to be, or who they expected themselves to be. To synchronise your mindset with your essential inner-being is the main challenge for all humans. This synchronisation is essential to fulfilling your life's purpose, aligning your sense of self with intent, thoughts, beliefs and values.

If success comes too easily the path has not been fully appreciated. It probably won't contribute much to your state of self-confidence, or create lasting satisfaction.

'Mastery experiences' are those you worked hard at and required real effort to achieve. Inherently, you derive satisfaction out of the process, not the perceived destination. In effect, you don't need rewards or admiration for your accomplishments, as the process itself fulfils that need. Being able to attentively apply yourself to the present moment, with joy, is rewarding in itself.

I used to imagine myself wining the EuroMillions lottery, especially when the jackpot pay-out was in excess of a hundred million pounds. Imagining what I would do was great fun, as my fleeting dreams included extravagant acquisitions and many exotic experiences. I would dream that I would have this 'superior' feeling of satisfaction, and then would become what I've always wanted to become. What I wanted was based on what I couldn't currently have, and projected future happiness. However I soon realised that I didn't want to feel superior to others, or show that I'm better than them. I also knew that fame and fortune would not bring me that future happiness I so longed for. Since then I've not played the lottery, as I'm not as enthusiastic about furthering my wait for the 'ship to come in'. I feel my ship has landed. She lands with every fraction of every moment that I'm aware of my fortunate existence in life. Success is sweet, yes. Even sweeter is the realisation that you are already surrounded by all the success you were looking for.

## Manifesting motivation

Have you ever been caught up in the moment, so severely that you lost track of time and space? Deep attention is one of the most satisfying experiences to be had, where nothing in the world matters anymore. These moments consist of extreme concentration, totally void of thoughts other than what you were focusing on. It empties the past or future mind, and with it all traces of emotions or wishes. These moments are directly linked to being absorbed in the present. This is also known as 'flow' and 'in the zone'. We are conceptually immersed in our work or activity to such an extent as to be truly productive and creative. Only by truly accepting the present state without distractions, do we not think about anything other than what's happening at that moment. In this way we become attentive to our directed thoughts, mentally accepting and succumbing to its pressing demands. We notice this happening especially with stressful deadlines, where urgent attention is required for high performance. Some people are able to turn this quality on and off by choice, despite the distractions. However this doesn't require superhuman qualities. All are capable of mastering this behaviour by practicing directed attention.

Attention in the current moment doesn't deviate into useless thought by itself.

It needs distractions to do so. Distractions come from anywhere, everywhere. They originate from fleeting thoughts or sensory inputs. Alternatively, attention is focusing despite disruptions, an acute awareness of what's presently happening. Without apparent emotional and conscious effort, consistent attentiveness gives us the means to achieve continual productive outcomes. Productive outcomes in turn are based on making present-time commitments. Concentrating on that 'one step at a time', according to Lao Tzu, you should savour each step fully. Each step should be made with full commitment, and as a muscle needs exercise, with practice the second step too becomes so much easier. Momentum is created where less and less motivation is required. By constantly reflecting on both the 'joy' of the path and the end result (for direction), the correct mindset will evolve. By systematically turning your tasks into tactics, you may then work towards broader and more challenging goals. Being intensely aware of attending deeply to a task (or another person), becomes a somewhat spiritual practice.

To increase motivation, contemporary psychologists tend to promote three actions: thinking positively, developing effective goals, and creating a conducive environment. Also, they profess the importance of the locus of control, which points to your mindset. You are the determiner of your circumstances. That is, you have to believe you are responsible for your success or failure. Positive thinking has been a controversial kitchen psychology subject for some time. It cannot be denied that our emotional status has a direct effect on our motivation, thus psychologists frequently comment on the required management of emotions and stress. However, one cannot simply state to yourself that you should be constantly optimistic and positive. This type of psychological self-indoctrination might aid your temporary state of mind, but essentially it's unrealistic to sustain. It doesn't take account of conflicting transient thoughts. Positive thinking habits often deny consideration and acceptance of the natural opposites in life. Life is full of paradoxes. Accepting and embracing our contradictory thoughts leads to valuable self-realisations. For example, when dealing with conceited characters, our predisposition is to become intolerant, resulting in our thoughts projecting an air of defensiveness or irritability. However, we instinctively know that this is unproductive, not benefiting either party. We feel we need to affirm our position, as to not 'lose face'. This way, our imposing egos can strengthen our feelings of self-worth, by justifying that we are 'right' and they are 'wrong'. This is just one example of the many paradoxes we must continuously face. The best way of dealing with emotions is to simply recognise them, and briefly ponder on the thoughts that caused them. Their causes are often derived from our misconceptions. Once we are aware of their origins they become less of a threat, and non-judgemental acceptance becomes possible. Then we are able to moderate our motivational levels. We will effectually be able to avoid mutual suffering.

Setting clear objectives is beneficial to working out a doable strategy to reach them. They should be clear, specific, realistic to achieve, and measurable. In business we often hear 'what cannot be measured, cannot be managed'. Yes, measuring progress toward an outcome is valuable, especially in terms of determining how much effort is allocated to reach certain milestones. These smaller milestone successes inspire us to move on with confidence. It becomes a virtual roadmap that shows us the way to stay on the straight and narrow. There is however another paradox here; sustained focus on objectives somewhat eliminates the wider scope of creativity and flexibility. We tend to close ourselves off to anything that doesn't fit our agenda, as the mind naturally cannot simultaneously concentrate on both. As we are gifted by both left and right brain anilities, we are also gifted in how we control our inherent balance of analytical and creative mindsets. We can and should switch frequently between both during our best efforts in whatever we do. This includes the processes of planning, strategizing, implementing and evaluating our achievements.

Conducive environments are also commonly mentioned by psychologists as beneficial to our motivational levels. Support from our surroundings enables the circumstances to stimulate self-development. Many excellent companies have realised that this aspect is crucial to remaining competitive, so as to keep and develop acquired talent. Does this mean that it's always necessary to have an ideal situation before we can become motivated? Not at all. Adequate intrinsic motivation isn't that much reliant on the outside environment. Motivation driven from your own conducive thoughts and emotions is best for your feeling of control. However, favourable working environments do influence internal thoughts and subsequent motivational levels somewhat. Some people are more susceptible to situational variations than others, as some rely more on external than internal factors. Sustaining high motivational levels, in spite of environmental conditions, is essentially the ideal psyche to achieve. This is done by the conscious acceptance of what is, and keeping your attention focused on present action initiatives.

When we go beyond our thinking, we don't give ourselves a chance to argue our way out of a commitment. We accept what is at that moment. We focus on being where we find ourselves, at that specific time. We don't need to think about what to do, or what should be done, we just 'do'. Typically though, our thoughts are either caught in the past or future, hardly ever in the present. When we think about any unfavourable situation, it's either anticipated from the future, or remembered from the past. Both situations can create excessive stress for us, and our thoughts of possible consequences often cause a dip in motivation. External factors should be seen as subjective, as it's our mind that translates these factors through the filter of our limited and fragile perceptions. Our perception of fear is often the 'imagined appearing real'. Fear is mostly formed by mind-made threats, either rationalised to others, or to yourself. Anticipating a situation where your comfort zone is compromised often brings fear and stress.

As unaware as fish are of water, similarly there would be no concept of 'motivation' if everyone was fully motivated. Motivation essentially falls away when one lives and works in the moment. By the way, I believe that fish primarily live in the moment! Motivational thought processes are only needed when we anticipate or expect, in other words when we think. In the moment, we attend to what is, and there's no motivation needed at all. When duly challenged, we can appreciate the pure motivational strength that comes across to the casual observer. That's why the experts make it looks easy. The powerful outcomes seen seem almost superhuman; however, they are the product of focus and attention, devoid of distracting thoughts.

CHAPTER 3

# Giving assurance: are you fascinated or are you frustrated?

*"Trust is the highest form of human motivation."*

Stephen R. Covey

## Pursuing your hospitality career

Choosing your career path seems like an enormous responsibility for any young person leaving school or university. It's certainly daunting trying to live up to everyone's expectations, not making major mistakes and confidently planning your path. Often undue pressure is put on young industry entrants to pursue that notorious ladder to progression quickly. Invariably many well-intended, but often ill-informed people are just too willing to offer their advice on this. Valuable information should be mindfully received and not necessarily acted upon. Realise this is your journey alone. No-one can walk it with you. This creates another paradox, where your need for autonomy conflicts with the burdening expectations of others. This tends to muddle our decision-making processes and creates much uncalled-for stress. Instead of opting for something unique, new entrants go low-risk, mainstream, or opt for indecisiveness. This might cause them to lose out on challenging opportunities. Playing it safe satisfies public opinion and appeases the naysayers, but hardly ever paves the path to accelerated self-discovery. It prohibits a higher level of thinking and constricts personal growth. Going beyond the comfort zone is frequently difficult to comprehend, for 'easier' is most seductive when things are uncertain or when our self-confidence is low.

During this confusing stage of life keep in mind there's not one, or a right, career path for anyone. Firstly, your path is unique, and though you might learn many things from your role-models, you can never simulate their path. You may also feel the need to design your own ideal path, and feel that it should work out as planned. Sorry to say, it never does. Life just has a way of dumping many messy trials and tribulations along your path. That doesn't mean you shouldn't plan. It merely means that you should see it for what it is: a map with a preferred path among many paths. It purely remains a rough guide. Inevitably, you will find yourself exactly where you should be, at any given time. What I mean is for you to find your ideal path, you need to accept the lessons that life gives you at any given moment. This will direct you to altered paths, with alternate outcomes. Much of what happens in your life only starts making sense in hindsight. However, to fulfil your destiny you need to stay focused on taking opportunity as it arises. It's less about making the right decision, and more about making 'a' decision. The path will eventually work out at it was meant to be, notwithstanding your wishes or expectations. Everything works out for the better when we are open to learning, and to experiencing new things. Problems often appear when we close our mindset, by convincing ourselves that we know it all. We habitually fool ourselves that we wouldn't appreciate something new and unknown, even though we've never tried it. Worse yet, if we did try something new without the right mindset, we might pre-emptively sabotage any worthy experience from it.

We never really stop learning, not subconsciously anyway. We are receptive to learning that we feel benefits us, even if it's not seen as beneficial by others. We convince ourselves within our thoughts that we know everything that we think is worth knowing. 'Fight or flight' stresses have historically manifested heightened awareness functions in humans, where receptive senses and thoughts process vital information most effectively. In modern times, this comes across as natural stress. When controlled effectively, it improves our learning curve and subsequent feelings of accomplishment when we achieve favourable outcomes. It spurs us on to do our best, pushing limits in order to either prove ourselves, or to gain approval. As I've seen of students in industrial placement, they often either embrace the limitations of their work environment, or else become defensive when challenged. It takes a smidgin of brainpower to see which one works out best. Choosing hospitality as a career is indeed a brave endeavour. It's not for the faint hearted or leisurely types. It's enough of a humbling experience to perpetually dent your ego. Further, it will provide you with endless enriching personal interactions, and many dreaded confrontations. It will, if the mindset has correctly been cultivated, provide a calling, not just a career. Most importantly, it will provide a purpose.

## The essential attributes, skills and competencies

You don't need to be extraordinarily gifted with remarkable talents or any specific traits to grasp and apply the ideal hospitality mindset. I frequently divulge to students the irrefutable but ubiquitous message that our industry really doesn't need rocket scientists. In fact, even business skills and formal qualifications aren't initially needed either. You will have ample opportunity to develop these skills as you progress further through your career. The most crucial of skills you can develop from the onset is gaining clarity about yourself, and where you would like to fit within the industry. How do you see yourself developing with particular purpose and intent? How will you find meaning in the work that you do, and how will do you develop the necessary mindset to get the most out of your given abilities? Particularly, how will you cultivate the hospitable mind to such an extent that you are consistently joyful and fully attentive? Throughout this chapter we will explore the trials and tribulations of making sense of the myriad of hospitality career options available. Hopefully, in preparing your exciting path to accomplishments, I will be able to assist you in making appropriate choices.

I believe we are all endowed with similar but dormant character traits that are similar to those in the highest performing professionals. Even though these traits are innate and somewhat developed socially throughout our formative years, some are practiced more than others. Dependent somewhat on our historical exposure to genetics and culture, we exhibit preferences for the development of some traits more strongly than others. We tend to use those traits that work for us more frequently, and through consistent practice, form habits that shortcut our thought, emotional processes and actions accordingly. As we have seen, good habits serve us well, and by utilising productive and beneficially automated triggers, they are strongly recommended to simplify our lives. Our brain neurones normally fire on regular pathways, making initial thought associations particularly difficult. This effectively keeps us in captivity within our customary thought patterns. This is why it's often difficult for us to break strong habits or be creative in our thinking. However, with concerted effort in relocating alternative patterns of thinking, time to time it becomes necessary to do so for personal growth. On our earthly journey adaptability is key to matching our mindset to the empirical world. As much as we want to curb bad habits, we would also like to increase our good habits, making them more entrenched within our lives and careers. For our competencies to shine through, consistent value-added actions are needed.

According to widespread research and human resource practitioners' opinions, accomplished soft skills and a favourable attitude to getting stuck in, are of the utmost importance when recruiting new entrants to the industry. Within operational levels of the organisation, recruitment preference is shown to be centred on demonstrably excellent customer relations, showing initiative, and being a team player. Within managerial levels, excellent employee-centred relations and being able to effectively manage organisational change are added to the equation. There's unanimity among industry captains about the need for employees with the 'right attitude', rather than technical skills. Additionally a strong work ethic and a capacity for sustained hard work are required. The posts most hard to fill are middle and senior management, chefs, and food-service staff.

Soft skills include qualities such as attitude, initiative, self-motivation, leadership, responsibility, communication, creative thinking, work ethic, teamwork, networking, decision-making, positivity, time management, motivation, flexibility, problem-solving, critical thinking, conflict resolution, ability to work under pressure, and negotiation. These skills are numerous, relatively abstract, and often difficult to become fully competent in. They are rather elusive to manage, or measure with any accuracy. In nature they are purely indicative of reality and can be mistakenly interpreted. They are often associated with misconceptions and biases. To be mindful and develop these skills effectively requires reflection on what these concepts mean to you personally. Clarity is key here, as the degree of self-knowledge will directly reflect in your competency level at these skills. Relating to the development of the mindset, some of the most important of these will be discussed during the course of the book. However I would urge you to become an avid reader on these 'soft skill' topics.

Transferable skills are general skills you can use in many different jobs, and include soft skills. You gain these skills from previous jobs, projects, voluntary work, sport, your home life, hobbies, and interests. They enable you to be adaptable and flexible in case you need to demonstrate your competencies in new situations. It's worth reflecting on transferable skills, as awareness of them within yourself builds self-confidence in your own capabilities. In practical terms, it's also desirable to illustrate your use of them within work applications and interviews. Employers will be impressed if you are able to provide tangible examples of when and how you used these skills effectively in previous jobs. This shows that you're adaptable and can bring useful skills to a job straight away. Please note that a skill is not the same as a task. Skills are something you use to produce results. Tasks or activities are something you do whilst at work. Results are relatively visible and measurable. Doing a task is visible, but cannot be measured for effectiveness unless there's a result. Therefore, it's a good idea to reflect, consistently document and gain evidence on how exactly your results contributed to your career progress and the company's goals.

## Reasons to study further

It fascinates me to listen to prospective students justifying their reasons for pursuing hospitality studies. Most of the reasons given are vague at best, though a few do get some coherent thought across as to their motivations. Most have not considered what 'hospitality' means to them, and typically reply with a non-descript truism, such as 'because I like people' or a similarly vague response. This certainly is a vital topic that needs your reflection in justifying purpose and career choices.

It's regularly apparent that the glamour of the hotel business appears at the forefront of hospitality careers. In other sectors of the tourism industry we also discover alluring and idyllic environments that have much potential in seducing us. Rarely considered are the 12-hour days, early shifts, the working weekends, and the holiday seasons dedicated to work. This career requires an unconventional social and family life. 'Expect the unexpected' is the key term here, as your hospitality career will probably be far removed from what you've initially imagined.

Seeing that formal education, and especially tertiary education, isn't a prerequisite for career progression, every Tom, Dick and Harry will be able to work themselves up the career ladder. I already hear those academically-focussed among you profusely protest at this fact. Yes, I do agree somewhat here. Indeed, education and technical skills cannot be totally ignored. They are necessary to properly understand the dynamics of business and technical processes when progressing through supervisory and managerial ranks. Controversial as it might seem, I believe some career success in our industry is indeed possible without formal education, though not usually probable for higher positions in current management. Notwithstanding, there's a considerable array of soft skills systematically augmented within higher education courses. As I am an academic coming from industry and used to conversing regularly with many captains of the trade, this point has spawned frequent discussions. No real conclusive evidence has ever been found with these matters; however, most end results have indicated that success was up to the candidate's mindset. This became clear: great education coupled with a poor grasp of essential soft skills and appalling attitude wouldn't effectively substitute for poor formal education, with great emotional intelligence, and a passionate attitude. The latter has undoubtedly proven to be far superior at every career level in hospitality.

Too few great candidates persist in the industry, which is a crying shame.

Hospitality jobs are seen as low status, often not as a serious career option for many. New entrants into the industry get discouraged by the seemingly poor work effort versus reward ratio. This is most prevalent in the lower operational ranks where pay is poor, and the required manual labour is especially intensive and thankless. It's a fact that many hospitality employees are in effect 'transient', doing a job merely as a means to earn a wage. They usually have a very different path planned, often not in hospitality. However, much needed part-time and temporary work is created this way, and the industry relies on this to control the fluctuations in demand over seasons. This obviously presents some challenges to the young career-seeking hospitality professional. They need to enter a cosmos of political turmoil, where many employees are uncommitted, and some in older and supervisory positions are often quite cynical. They may, too, be set in their self-righteous ways. On the other hand, this scenario might provide generous opportunities to flourish, showcase young ambitions, evolve latent talent and enhance positive mindsets. These types of environment will happily provide one with ample educational challenges, by being able to exercise one's skills, and to encourage you to take charge and show that you can be trusted to lead. Stepping up to any task is the quickest way to be recognised as managerial potential. The hospitality workplace is a virtual playpark of considerable skill-development opportunities, and should be embraced with enthusiasm. Whatever you need to learn, you can learn within the immediate environment. This is best illustrated by examples of how the lowest-tiered employees can achieve huge success, as numerous company presidents have famously illustrated, working themselves up from humble beginnings. There's often no better training than on the job itself. However, this can only be regarded as value-added if it is consciously approached by the participant with awareness.

A conscious approach to your work means not just paying attention to what you do, but reflecting on why and how you accomplish tasks. Remaining aware of your state of mind while performing tasks is vital in getting the most value from what you are learning, and in doing things properly. Gaining 'flow', as previously discussed, is the attentive focus that you bestow on a customer and a task. For that to be sustainable, you need to stay in the present moment, and not get distracted by intrusive thoughts or by outside occurrences. Consistency in this mindful practice will ensure a blissful work and life experience.

There are chronic shortages of good managerial talent, and that alone is good reason to study hospitality and/or business sciences. Tertiary education is a suitable shortcut to working yourself up through the ranks. Given the right mindset, the investment in any education is always worth it. Higher education is indicative of a higher level of critical thinking, problem-solving and conceptualising practical and theoretical issues. Qualifications of this nature are favoured for top managerial positions in industry. Each country, culture and sector has various industry needs in terms of preferred qualifications. I will not discuss this topic in detail as the book's theme relates to mindsets. Your educational desires need to be effectively matched with future industry requirements and personal ambitions. Positioning yourself accurately needs to be properly researched. It often seems as though prospective students have very little idea of the myriad career paths available, except for the typical and stereotyped job titles. With a little creative forethought and research, we will soon notice new industry positions trending because of the technologies invented, and the specialised operating knowledge and experience that is increasingly required. I've seen the most resourceful of young practitioners getting involved with industry via professional organisations, conferences, associations, and networks to maximise their exposure to current and future trends. This involvement doesn't just facilitate useful contacts and knowledge, but most importantly provides opportunities and clarity of purpose. Subsequently, with more exposure and awareness of opportunities comes a holistic view of yourself, your capabilities and your role within hospitality. From a human resource point of view, you are then able to properly cultivate the right mindset to propel yourself into the ideal job position.

## Generalisation vs specialisation

Buckminster Fuller aptly said, 'we are in an age that assumes the narrowing trends of specialisation to be logical, natural, and desirable… In the meantime, humanity has been deprived of comprehensive understanding. Specialisation has bred feelings of isolation, futility, and confusion in individuals. It has also resulted in the individual's leaving responsibility for thinking and social action to others. Specialisation breeds biases that ultimately aggregate as international and ideological discord, which in turn leads to war.'

This could easily be interpreted as an extreme view on the issue of specialisation; however, it contains clear snippets of truth, even for the most ardent cynic amongst us. The views reflected in the quote remain indicative of our common states of mind; of division, differentiation, labelling and individualism. Once again, as with all debatable issues in life, another paradox appears here. Generalist views require wide-scope thinking, with many ambiguous priorities leading to situations where you might spread yourself too thin. Therefore you're able to devote attention only fractionally and sporadically. On the other hand, specialisation requires full attention on a few main priorities, which increases productivity and thus the subsequent effects are much more pronounced. Alternatively, while a holistic and generalist outlook is inclusive, communal, and about breaking down barriers, specialisation is more about staking your claim, self-development, uniqueness, and separation. Both paradigms have their own virtues and drawbacks, and each individual will have various levels of these disparate qualities. Nevertheless, we need to devote some of our time and effort to both perspectives to properly cultivate and suitably balance the mindset.

As we are commissioned to play certain 'roles' in life and career, it's best that we prepare fully for them. Ideally, formal and informal life-long learning should be pursued. Learning in all its dimensions should focus in accordance with the direction of our attention. Our attention is a powerful tool indeed. As our thoughts process the past and present subjects of attention, these thought perceptions are given meaning, understanding, emotions and belief. They subsequently form our values, which underlie all human behaviour. While acting out the myriad roles in our lives, we need to realise that these roles are not 'us'. These roles are tangible representations of our existence in this world. They are labels given to us, by ourselves and others. We are, in fact, very different from the roles we present. We have the ability to change roles, change our behaviour, and change our attention at any given time. We can even change our perceptions of the past, modifying how it appears to us within our minds. This suggests that we can effectively control our minds. Nevertheless most of humanity is convinced that their minds and external circumstances have control over them and the state of their lives. Thus, to illustrate the critical balance between specialisation and generalisation, we need to understand the relational interdependence of both, and how our attention applies it to our experiences.

Interpreting our daily environment and other people holistically is imperative to breaking down social barriers. Being non-prejudicial towards our customers leads to excellent service. Likewise team-building, effective leadership and self-efficacy require a generalist understanding of psycho-demographical attributes and high-end communication skills. However we are just as capable of sustaining pin-sharp focus on specific areas of our talent and interest at any given time, by directing our attention to the subject. Controlling our minds at will, we are able to simultaneously focus on the same customer without prejudice (generalism), and with intended focus (specialism). The same applies to functional areas of industry specialisation. Becoming proficient at all subject matters or skills is practically impossible. We just don't have the mental capacity to do so. We are all given a finite range of time, physical and mental ability. We need to free up as much mind-space as possible to devote our mental capacity to focus. Any prejudiced thought fills much needed mind-space, thus distracting us from what we should be attending to.

We always have the opportunity to prioritise, and we do so by giving something attention. We should become conscious of how, and to what, we give attention. What are the ramifications of not using our attention optimally? Without attention, we cannot be aware, and without awareness we won't be able to see the bigger picture. Thus specialism is reliant on generalism, and vice-versa. These are two sides to the same coin. Paradoxically, with deeper understanding of a subject, we come to realise that we know very little indeed, that everything is infinite in its depth. There's no last word on anything. It's this realisation that opens us up for further discovery and life-long learning. Wisdom means knowing that we cannot truly know anything, including ourselves. The state of not knowing leads to a child-like fascination with all we come in contact with, like seeing things for the first time. This is the essence of true attention: seeing old things from afresh, without presumptions and preconceived ideas. Thus, to conclude, both specialisation and generalisation are required to perceive, learn and think with a hospitable mindset. Instead of becoming frustrated by what we don't know, knowledge of the specifics within the general provides us with that sense of wonder and the awe of naivety.

## Proficiency as a manager

Contrary to what everyone else says to you, you will be required to demonstrate managerial qualities from the first day on the job. Even though you might be appointed in an operational capacity, it will still be expected that you demonstrate generalist hospitality skills. These might include excellent communication, leading by example, building effective teams, organisational skills, and emotional intelligence. Note how many soft skills are conditional here: all of them! The extent to which you're able to demonstrate proficiency in these areas will determine the trust others will have in your ability to take on a supervisory role. You will need to embrace responsibility for influencing positive attitudes, and projecting a high level of enthusiasm and energy. You will need to impart consistent encouragement and constructive criticism where and when necessary.

We are most positively influenced by strong role-models, and we are most likely to sustain our motivational levels if the role model accurately reflects our existing or desired value system. Seeing how they have accomplished their purpose benefits us in learning from their experience. However, there are no short-cuts to being fulfilled within work and life. A suitable input will most likely lead to a suitable output, and a satisfactory result. True success without the required effort is almost impossible, and if by any chance it should happen, a hollow victory it would be indeed. Being unfulfilled by your efforts will feed your conscious as well as your subconscious mind with negative thoughts and emotions, leading to diminished self-worth. Unconditional and full acceptance of the challenges that precede the fruits of labour and the required effort is worth it most of the time.

Being 'in charge' is a label typically given to managers. Being in control is very satisfying to the excessive ego, as it mentally confirms to you that you are superior to others. Power often corrupts, as the saying goes, with well-meaning leaders abusing the authority given to them. We see this too often in politics, the military, religion, and in hospitality, among other facets of life. With any managerial and leadership roles come responsibilities, some privileges and a significant price to pay. This needs to be reflected upon holistically, for it needs to be assimilated with your purpose. The saying 'if you can't take the heat, get out of the kitchen' is apt here, as acknowledgement and acceptance of your chosen role is crucial in determining your lifestyle and career path. Ambitious as you are, you might possibly be tempted to display some healthy confidence in the workplace. Nevertheless, it's also essential to incorporate a good moderating dose of humility. Humility is generally described as a state of being humble, modest, lacking pretence, and not having a belief that you are superior to others. It implies directing the ego away from focussing solely on oneself, and extending your awareness to others. Firstly, this means that the ego needs to be identified for what it is: a made-up identity with self-constructed contexts within a self-perceived history. This ego needs to feed off affirmations of encouragement, labels and importance. Humility, however, is about embracing the worth, not just of oneself, but also of others. On occasion we see highly accomplished professionals who are high on the humility index, typically those who achieve the most, brag the least. They are the most valued role models. The more secure they are in themselves, the more humble they become. It's an essential precursor to participative management to see yourself as equal to others, but most importantly to see yourself in service of others. This is the essence of the hospitable mind. Humility is a meta-virtue. This means it participates dynamically in all of your life's roles. For example, it is demonstrated in the treatment of others no matter who they are, as well as your attitude in approaching tasks with an open mind. You shouldn't think you know it all, for the basic fact is that you don't. Nobody does. If you were truly mindful, you wouldn't be influenced by an arrogant, self-centred, and egotistical manager. Alternatively, humility opens up possibilities, enhances open-mindedness and curiosity, and diminishes self-serving opinions. In conclusion, humility facilitates the ideal environment for motivation to flourish.

## Managing the work environment

Expecting the work environment to cater to our needs is somewhat unrealistic. This environment, like all others, has evolved with a purpose in mind. It doesn't necessarily reflect your purpose as such. The overarching purpose of commercial business is realising company growth and profits. The agents to facilitate this growth, like you and your colleagues, are merely instrumental in the bigger scheme of things. However, this somewhat cynical view is valuable in creating context within your mindset, as you will have to see the work environment for what it is: another stage role in the production of life. You are paid a regular reward to function in an appointed position within a commercial concern, to add to the efforts of others in order to serve the commercial goals of the company. The sustainable business model proposes that 'the total should be more than the sum of its parts'. This suggests that you are indeed viewed as an investment when you function optimally, and your output is likely to be more valuable than your input.

This is sometimes a tough reality to face as we get more acquainted with our environment: we develop sentiments and attach emotions to our environments based on our expectations and subsequent experiences. If the environment plays out according to our expectations, we attach higher levels of trust, goodwill and loyalty to it. When circumstances don't work out so well, we experience the environment as restrictive, hostile and less conducive to satisfying our expectations. Although many of these feelings originate in environmental factors, our preconceived thoughts, with the associated emotions and attitudes, have a phenomenal influence on how we experience the quality of our work. There's a concept called 'motivated reasoning', where logical deduction is used to defend a preferred position already favoured by the mindset. This is when we are able to think, say or act defensively, without considering the full picture. We are prone to blaming the situation on others to justify our thoughts and feelings. This strengthens our ego, and makes it easier to walk away, shedding any further responsibility. Nothing gets solved that way, and you will be taking the mental baggage with you wherever you go. Conversely, we find that 'open-minded reasoning' sheds those preconceived notions, and tries to remain unbiased. Instead of frustration, caused by feeling restricted, you feel intrigued, curious, even fascinated by the challenging work environment.

So, how do we remain unbiased? Is it even possible? The holistic mindset is like a muscle that needs consistent strengthening. To get the full picture of a situation involves us not just being emotionally intelligent; it needs us to be aware and attentive. Being aware is the gateway to remaining unbiased and non-judgemental. Preconceived thoughts indicate expectations. Your expectations are made up from your historical stories and life-long perceptions of what is acceptable to you or not. Realising that 'acceptance' is a decision we make that we're not accepting any restriction, is key here. For that to happen, you need to let go of your restrictive thoughts by recognising the intrusive past thoughts you have accumulated. I say here 'recognising', not avoiding or scorning those thoughts. They are useful tools in making sense of the world; however, they restrict our attention span. Our attention needs to be present to think without prejudice, without expectations. That's where awareness comes in: we are able to recognise our thoughts as separate objects that come and go through our consciousness. As we become aware and notice them, with their attached emotions, they will eventually dissipate. Our thoughts about a person or situation are recalling labels we've posted and accumulated. We could term a person as 'arrogant', or the situation as 'unacceptable' according to current experiences based on previous perceptions. This was 'true' to us in the past, and now has a good chance of being 'true' once again, as our minds have already built in the bias. Even if it were empirically true, which philosophically it can't be, it destroys the value of the present moment experience. Thoughts are ego-based, and as such viscously defend, justify and protect the identities we have created. We compulsively have the need to feel we are right, and not to be shown we could be wrong.

An example of this was when I worked in a hotel on the border of East and West Jerusalem, at the height of the second 'Intifada' (uprising) of the Palestinians against the Jewish community. It was a very volatile period for both Jews and Arabs. Having preconceived ideas about working with Palestinians, I was confronted by my own bias. Not being particularly mindful about my prejudices, I had many confrontations come my way, which challenged my initial cultural opinions. You can choose to ignore these signs, or embrace them by accepting them fully and incorporating openness in your mindset. I stubbornly denied my own part in my strife, and resorted to becoming defensive, laying blame on others. I felt they did not understand me or appreciate me. In time I came to realise that this wasn't true or wise, and eventually got the message, loud and clear. I had to realise that the ignorance of others had no bearing on my own. By projecting my insecurities upon them, I didn't improve the situation at all. However, with time I became aware of their state of mind, and I understood the threat they perceived when I invaded their workspace uninvited. I should have been more aware, more attentive of others' mindsets. This means recognising that they are just as trapped in their minds as anyone else. Therefore they too are subject to their own psychological makeups. Since then I've endeavoured to not react, but respond immediately with attentiveness and kindness. I try not to expect, and avoid prejudice to others, as much I could.

Besides our internal mindset, fellow colleagues and especially managers seem to matter a lot in creating a conducive and motivational work environment. Contemporary research shows that hospitality managers usually express the importance of having the right team 'spirit' as well as having an 'enthusiastic' social atmosphere. Similarly, and in line with the required soft skills, it also indicates the importance of attitudes, inclusion and the enthusiasm of the managers toward their lower-level colleagues. Incorporating these qualities becomes much easier by holistically accepting your work environment, warts and all. This doesn't mean that you become complacent about whatever challenging situations might arise, but this mindset provides you with the necessary clarity regarding all that happens, with proper perspective. Being open-minded and focussed on the issues that matter, without preconceived ideas, is a blueprint for being a great manager. Creating an environment of trust is imperative for progressive business practices, and this can only be achieved once barriers are taken down. Where all participants feel they matter, and where transparency is entrenched throughout, then employees are regarded more than their labels would indicate. This all stems from real communication, more connection, and tolerance for individual differences.

Unfortunately work environments aren't always ideal. We have to contend with many objectionable elements, and coping with troubled co-workers is just one of them. Toxic workers are a 'double-negative' when determining the potential costs to a company. Besides not being productive, they also escalate social inertia within the company culture, undermining general productivity and cooperation. Yet we cannot let dire circumstances dictate our behaviour, and these are those times when we are challenged to rise above them. By remaining aware and attentive to doing our best within the present moment, and not prey by the second-hand thoughts of others, we deter and deflect much of the negative energy directed towards us. This is, in effect, the way company cultures are altered. By means of being an example with positive influence, others who might be adversely instigated are pacified, by following role models of tolerance. Particularly as you enter the industry, leaders will be watching closely how you fit in. They'll be scrutinising the attitude and initiative you bring, as well as your cooperation with colleagues.

The demand for high-performing staff is well-known, so close examination of your work ethics by others will certainly follow. The Ritz-Carlton training manual famously states, 'We are ladies and gentlemen serving ladies and gentlemen'. This is in regards to their employees projecting and receiving equal respect in the work environment. It's important to remember that with any given service function, serving people or organisations isn't lowering yourself in relation to others. The most powerful and legendary of leaders serve: whether their country, their constituents, their companies, or any other cause or being. This is universal, even though many dictators might not recognise this fact. To serve is to project yourself outwards with confidence to others, and to a greater cause than yourself. Hint: this will have much to do with your purpose, as earlier discussed. Inevitably you will then earn the respect you so rightly deserve. However, you shouldn't rely on receiving this respect; you will know your value internally, even if others don't. To serve is to lead. And so, too, to lead is to serve. You, as leader or servant, have called yourself to action by realising the intrinsic value of serving someone or something else. You have recognised the human being behind the labels and roles. You have an awareness of the prejudiced thoughts that cross your mind; and that they have no effect on your attention toward this person. You are wholly in the present, taking charge of what needs to be done at any given moment. Then you realise, that this is the essence of the hospitable mind.

## Bringing it all together: EQ, IQ, skills, and competencies

Directing yourself toward a suitable career path is fairly simple, in my opinion. We tend to complicate simple matters because of our fears and preconceived ideas. We tend to over-analyse and over-think everything to a premature death. There's no exact science for career choice; however, many books have been written on the subject, many of which are very valuable. In a nutshell, all you need to do is reflect on your personal values, set your purpose, determine your strengths and weaknesses, envision your lifestyle, see how you can make a contribution to the industry by researching suitable opportunities, and finally decide what position you will need to fill to accomplish your personal goals. Simple indeed! You don't need to get it totally right, as very few people ever do. The idea is to have as much fun (with your clothes on) as possible, during your lifetime of discovery. Your path should follow a fluid and flexible plan that calls for perpetual reformatting to remain effective. Still, you shouldn't be fixated too much on reaching your goals, to the detriment of not noticing alternative opportunities. Do 'smell the roses along the way'. Being singularly focussed on outcomes takes much of the fun and spontaneity of life away. It gives way to narrow-mindedness, self-righteousness and closed mindsets. Your career path is similar to the rest of your life, and represents a chosen growth process. As such, your experiences along the way need ample time, maturity, wisdom and patience to fully develop and to be thoroughly enjoyed.

Our ideal working environment is one of complex dynamics, where we would like to be appropriatcly challenged to stretch ourselves for growth. However it's imperative to also feel included, valued, and appreciated. We like to be part of a larger system that follows the same values as us. Occasionally we love to get behind collective causes or projects we believe in. Subjectively we have this constant push and pull feeling where, on one side, inertia must be overcome, and on the other, performance flows freely. Oh, and the dread of Monday mornings when you need to drag your sorry self to work. However, once you get on a productive roll, the week seems to become better. At work we tend to play specific roles which are usually very different to our other roles in life. We literally take on, and act out, those labels bestowed upon us as our identity. That's who we become. Accordingly our personas change with what these roles represent. We need to realise that roles and labels are there to serve us, there to make sense of our workplace, and that they are merely practical tools for specific circumstances. Problems arise when we believe that this is who we are, and we incorporate that role (with associated labels and personas) into other facets of life.

Many a time we see stressed executives heading home from work, and playing the same role at home as at work; becoming commanding, overbearing and self-important towards family members. Often when someone acts like that, they aren't aware of their behaviour. It's unconsciously integrated within their persona and thought processes, which they literally identify with. In reality they are none of the roles they assume, as none of them point to their actual identity. You must understand that 'you' are beyond your thoughts, roles and labels. In general, this is what most people fail to recognise. Intellectually it's rather complex to grasp. Even if you're fortunate enough to understand the concept, in practice it's difficult to apply consistently to everyday life. Even though you are intimately involved in playing your role, you still need to realise that you are acting. The actor isn't you; it's only a projection of you. Thus, remain conscious of the role you take on, and how you play it out. This is where the reflection of your soft skills needs to be carefully articulated. Are you confident that you have chosen the correct roles for your career and life?

We tend to underrate ourselves in terms of what we are able to accomplish, what we are able to do, and what we would like to do. Human beings have an enormous capacity to willingly adapt to the most catastrophic of situations. We don't know what we don't know, and we secretly fear it immensely. Even if we knew what to fear, our biased mindsets will anticipate a similar known situation to appear. Our preconditioned thoughts will inevitably repeat. It's as though we unconsciously long for that 'déja-vu'. Our minds thrive on the familiar. However when we play our roles with awareness, we're mindful of their influence and energy. Similarly we're mindful in getting the best out of ourselves and others to accomplish results. Playing our roles in the present moment, giving attention in conducting ourselves with integrity, makes us accepting of others without judgement. Don't focus so much on outcomes, as this will sometimes bring distraction in the form of disparaging thoughts about the future. Results will come when you do things properly in the present moment. In other words, know your goals, but don't focus on them. Your full attention towards the current passage of time is crucial.

Do we recognise our traits as part of ourselves, or as a thoughts separate from us? Traits are an accumulation of behaviour patterns that are seen to form part of our personality and character. They are also known as characteristics. These traits cleverly disguise themselves as part of the 'self' we identify ourselves with. Our egos need to maintain and rationalise the 'self' identity, and be continuously fed with thoughts on how we are doing. Frequent mixed and opposing messages race through our minds as to our state of our performance: 'am I assertive enough?' 'Ha, I told her so...', or 'I need more confidence', or 'why did she take advantage of me? Am I too friendly?' When we gloat over, ridicule or exploit others with what we perceive as our strengths (which may well be perceived as weaknesses by others), we feed our insatiable egos. Egos are necessary for functioning properly as human beings, and are thus imperative for performance and achievement. However, by being aware of the ego's ferocious appetite and strong tendencies to self-righteousness, we can moderate its negative effect in our lives. This starts with recognising those intruding thoughts that play out negatively in our assumed roles. We recognise the thought patterns which launch linked traits. For example, when we are criticised, and by chance happen to have low self-esteem, we could over-compensate on defence and act aggressively on impulse. We should realise and acknowledge the traits as they come to the surface. We could then admit and accept them. In this way we diminish the strength of our intensifying ego and effectively moderate our behaviour accordingly. So, in order to understand and empower ourselves better, we need to remain aware that our customary thought patterns deceptively manifest within our minds, disguised as true reality. See your thoughts as house guests: they are mostly welcome, and can be entertained with due hospitality and appreciated. But don't let them misbehave, overstay their welcome, or most importantly, never let them rule the house.

## Future trends

What does the future require of a leader in hospitality? My Strategy professor at the hotel school in Lausanne, Mike Olsen (now passed) wrote a list that remains, in my opinion, a rather accurate prediction throughout the years. He mentioned a multifunctional manager, thinking like a strategist, with fewer craft skills, and more business skills. Further he mentions being a 'change agent', by spanning boundaries beyond your obvious job description. Additionally, being visionary, a technologist, a knowledge worker as well as an information manager. You will need to be capable of analysing and synthesising incredible amounts of information, which includes guests, internal operations, and external data. You will also need innovative leadership skills to motivate a more knowledgeable and diverse work force: quite daunting, but a great challenge.

As most readers of this book will likely be Generation Y or Z, this is especially relevant to them: they will have to manage their careers much more actively, constantly thinking, 'what's the next move?' They will also be having shorter bites of experience, as frequent job changes will be the norm. Higher education is continuing to struggle to provide young people with relevant (read: soft) skill sets. Diverse and new careers are continuously added to industry. I'm looking forward to many new industry careers which haven't been invented yet. Universities are usually slow in responding to industry trends in terms of educational programmes; however, hotel schools are more technically aligned with the industry's functional requirements. Schools and universities are still teaching our young to become institutionalised and follow instructions, yet the global economic demand is moving in a different direction. The market increasingly requires creative and flexible work environments, with improved independent input. Business ecosystems are progressively becoming open, networked, collaborative, and transparent. There's a decrease in the predispositions for following instructions handed down in a rigid, hierarchical fashion, and an increase in testing new ideas with peers globally. Borders and boundaries mean much less to the younger generations, who are actively pushing beyond them with the aid of new technology.

No matter what the future holds for industry, the fundamentals of the hospitality mindset will stay the same. However many challenges may face the industry, from artificial intelligence to automation, the essential human participation (in some form) will prevail. Once the purpose of hospitality is internalised within the professional's mindset, the base is firmly set for any developments that might be required. No matter what the external circumstances might involve, the 'internal compass' remains intact. Using the compass as an illustration, the internal spindle stays central, irrespective of which direction the magnetic needle is pointed. This is the true self, the unchangeable self that all beings possess. The compass base also remains steadfast, by supporting the spindle, its needle and housing – this could be seen as your mindset. The ever-changing magnetic coordinates indicated by the needle identify the exchangeable roles we continuously play to give outward direction to our lives. A proper approach to our hospitable mindset is achieved when our destination, needle and magnetic coordinates are aligned.

## CHAPTER 4

# Being empathetic: are you caring or are you indifferent?

*"Now, hello, please know this. Humanity cannot be faked. Caring cannot be faked. Gratitude cannot be faked. Most people are too smart for that, and everyone eventually smells out a phony."*

Suzy Welch

## Caring, value and gratitude

An essential ingredient for the hospitable mindset is the 'care factor', probably one of the most undervalued and taken-for-granted attributes within the industry. It is prevalent in most companies' mission statements, but mostly given lip-service for all main stakeholders. Very few practitioners contemplate what it essentially means, and how it should be demonstrated as part of their company ethos. Undoubtedly everyone in the service industry has their own concept of what care consists of, and the required practice needed to exercise it within their job functions. Within this chapter we will reconsider the care factor, how it should fit into our mindsets in order to enhance the quality of our connections with others. I'll be highlighting the most pertinent of considerations that have worked for me and those that I've been fortunate to coach, without getting into much theoretical analysis. Related concepts are discussed so that you can form a clearer framework of the complexities that exist around this significant psychological topic.

We know by now that our conditioned mind takes empirical reality, then distorts these perceptions via our senses into thought so as to make sense to us. This we need to do in a functional world to accomplish our ideals: to categorise, to associate feelings with, and to label. It has been found that innate feelings of caring exist within all beings. Different cultures create different expressions of compassion, empathy, and other forms of psychological affinity toward others in need. Even though the care factor is natural within all humans, it's widely recognised that it's also a part of learned behaviour. Therefore it's generally viewed as a quality that can be cultivated further. Indeed we recognise that many legendary figures, past and present, have demonstrated selflessness, such as Mother Theresa, the Dalai Lama, and Nelson Mandela. Somehow these figures have managed to centre their lives' mission according to a 'care factor', which compliments and underpins all their other values. As such, it's logical that the thoughtful incorporation and development of this trait becomes of utmost importance within the hospitable mindset. Unconsciously, many take caring for granted as an innate quality, and usually don't give it a second thought. Recognising that this trait is more substantial and fundamental than mere behaviour is crucial for us to adopt a reflective attitude towards it. In other words, we shouldn't resign its significance to a mere superficial feeling, as unfortunately so many industry practitioners do. There's substance in becoming aware of the care factor. It has the potential to deeply impact our lives.

So, how do we re-appreciate caring? How do we bestow the necessary care unconditionally within our workplace, not just toward others, but also toward our environments? Caring relates directly to our attitude. The more valuable we deem something to be, the more we will be caring towards it. However, seeing something as 'valuable' is somewhat problematic, as any empirical reality is obviously subject to individual perspective and appreciation. The value of anything is derived from our historical stories, and therefore ambiguous and thought-dependent. We are taught (or not!) about respect and care for, among others, life, animals, and people, especially babies and the elderly. These views were, in turn, imbedded by the similarly constrained perspectives of our parents, teachers, peers and others who were influential in our lives. Therefore we should recognise their inherent limitations, however well they may have served us in our lives thus far. Recognising these social, communal and cultural limiting effects makes us aware of our own limiting nature, how we perceive 'care' and what it means to us.

Generally, it's easy to care for those close to us, as the value is explicit to the benefit derived. With friends and family we tend to be more relaxed in displaying a wider scope of traits, good, bad or indifferent. We are also often able to safely display unacceptable or rude behaviour within close social circles, as these traits are more readily accepted by them. Similarly we also establish more intimate connections with friends, partners or family. They thus remain a safe space of expression for us. However, we often feel as though we can't express ourselves truthfully to others, as the role-playing we try to sustain can sap much of our creativity, psychological health and energy. Remaining authentic requires courage and confidence. We tend to presume that taking on a role that others expect us to play, smooths over the communication process and appeases all participants. Roles are by nature mindset-based, thus variable by design, as they are an accumulation of traits with a label that identifies us to others. A way to moderate the variability of traits is to establish clear values, of which 'caring' can be of huge importance to the hospitality practitioner. Roles subject to well-developed values provide more consistency in behaviour and perspectives during decision-making. Caring as a fundamental value is central to developing the traits and associated behaviours we need in performing our hospitable tasks effectively, with due substance.

With caring we need to recognise the value of all beings and experiences we come across in our lives. Nothing has no value, and therefore everyone and everything is invaluable. Realise again that the 'value' label is a mind-made fabrication. Our theoretical labels term some things more valuable than others, therefore creating differentiations such as status, importance and priority. Care as a fundamental value cannot be conditional or prejudicial. It can only be applied by the human mind in terms of worldly context, and is therefore theoretical. Traits, emotions, and behaviour are mostly conditional to whatever they are applied to, as individual mental paradigms differ widely. However, with the awareness of an enlightened insight, we are able to strengthen our minds sufficiently to obtain and consistently ingrain the caring factor. This awareness should ensure that a basic value system conducive to serving others effectually can be within reach. Authenticating the inherent trait of caring lays an essential foundation; it is one of the primary values of the hospitable mindset.

Understanding care and empathy requires going beyond the apparent to a concept more primordial. The concept that corroborates such an intellectual basis is 'gratitude'. Gratitude is often seen as a forgotten muscle that needs to be exercised, to be fully appreciated. When we are grateful, we also care about the forces of nature which have provided so much for us. It enables us to recognise the contributions of seemingly insignificant everyday effects from others. Randomness as a principle disappears, and we notice the effectual link of all that happens around us. The slightest acts of goodwill have positive repercussions far beyond human comprehension. Unfortunately, so do acts of inhumane behaviour. Objects and processes in this world are forms of art, created by all people, acquired and cared for to bring us their very nature, for our own use in some way. Everyday occurrences and things we encounter are there to contribute to our lives, be they seen as 'good' or 'bad'. They are exactly as they should be, at the time, and at the specific place. They are never random or luck. Everything that happens has a reason, which often isn't realised at the time.

Sometimes such occurrences can only be explained in retrospect, and often they cannot be explained unless gratitude is appreciated.

The challenges we are fortunate to encounter are our spiritual teachers in life's trials and tribulations. As we grow psychologically and become spiritually aware, we realise that all the things that happen in life are pointers. They teach our mindsets the way forward and onward. Our awareness evolves, as all humans' inherent contributions become clear to us. When we notice that all occurrences or people aren't inherently good or bad, we essentially capture the essence of gratitude. Just being part of this miracle of life begs our gratitude; being able to experience it is amazing. We usually take this for granted. Key here is the understanding that our innate caring trait is indicative of our gratitude towards others. We must appreciate others' part in us making sense of our worldly experience. They, and all of creation, are our spiritual teachers in guiding our awareness.

As youngsters, most of us must have experienced a remark from our parents along the lines of, 'Please eat all your food; you don't know how privileged you are! You could have been starving as many kids across the world do.' This example attempts to illustrate how interdependent caring and gratitude is: where the awareness of others' subsistence living arouses in our minds the value of caring. Therefore it should simultaneously encourage our sense of gratitude for what we have, and have received. However, if the caring and gratitude are from different contexts, and especially if the scenarios are contextually far apart, it doesn't quite work as a linked mental association. For caring to be closely associated with gratitude, we need to create the closest mental connection between the two. A better example would be if you said, 'Please eat all your food. Poor Mandy in year 3 had to line up with her mother for lunch at the "Meals on Wheels" outside the library today. I hope she had enough to eat.' The child can now identify more closely with Mandy's situation, and easily feel what she might be feeling. Thus more closely connected contexts are created, and caring can now be directly associated with gratitude by the child.

'Waiter...waiter, there's a fly in my soup!' This proverbial joke example from industry illustrates the typical guest complaint. The guest's apparent position is quite reasonable in that he expects the meal that he purchased to be produced according to clear specifications, without unwanted additions. Nevertheless, it's not essentially about the 'fly' or the 'soup'. Besides these obvious technical inadequacies, what the guest really expects here is a basic but important element of acknowledgement. The guest first and foremost wants someone to recognise his presence. Therefore, regardless of product failures, as hospitality practitioners, we always need to empathise and recognise the guest as a fellow human being, before moving on to any further technical solutions. The nature of this acknowledgement comes across as a calm, open-minded and attentive awareness. Awareness frees up mental space within the initiator (waiter) and likewise absorbs the disturbed energy from the respondent (guest). This mental state then smooths the path for further receptiveness and effective action. We should accomplish this type of open-minded connection without mental constructs. Any guest dissatisfaction is to be recognised without presumption, and therefore demonstrated by observing them intently. This is how we acknowledge someone's presence. Realise that within the 'moment of truth' we should be grateful for the exclusive opportunity to serve others, thereby to contribute in resolving guests' dissatisfactions. We essentially gain more value from this than the people we serve. Giving really is more valuable than receiving. It makes us focus beyond ourselves, our insatiable egos, and our hyped-up temporary identities. For something that we attend to outside ourselves, it goes beyond the 'me'. It therefore becomes a cause which you can make your own cause. A cause is a focussed, goal-orientated effort combined with conviction and energy. It's powerful, and typically it's not self-serving. With a strong cause you can't help but care, often to the detriment of the identified self. Frequently the personal self, the ego, fundamentally becomes irrelevant, as many a true spiritual leader has illustrated. Here we recognise the value of caring: the unconditional receptiveness of the 'giving' mindset, accompanied by expressing of gratuity for those opportunities that present themselves as a worthy cause.

When we are confronted with the needs of others, do we respond to them or shy away? What creates the psychological inertia we so often experience, delaying our decision to act? Caring takes courage, as there's a worrying quality of vulnerability present when we display due care toward others. Being gentle with ourselves is often daunting enough, as it's often easier to scorn our own misbehaviours than others'. Being gentle with ourselves and others feels like we are somehow diminishing ourselves. In some ways, we are. The excessive ego, which strengthens itself even more by being superior to others, says, 'I can't lower myself to this person's level to show I care…' These ego-driven responses create the conditions for inertia to flourish. We become reluctant to allow ourselves to reach out towards another's psyche in need. When we become aware and consciously let go of our ego's prejudiced thoughts, the conditions are created to sort out this 'motivational conflict' we might experience. This motivational conflict happens when both caring and selfish thoughts coexist in the mind; this mindset paradox needs to be resolved for us to effectively move to action. Awareness of our conflicting thoughts must be observed for what it is, without judgement, as it's quite natural. Egos always put their selves first, and simply recognising this mental trait liberates us from the attachment to it. It's only there when you find it, not when you seek it: you can only observe your thoughts as they happen, and you cannot prevent them from happening. In other words you don't have to wait for those thoughts, they will come regardless. All you have to do is to remain open enough to notice. Like anything else substantial, it needs practice to become aware.

As mentioned, the 'why' is a precursor to the 'how'? Why should we care? One needs to mentally preconceive the personal benefits of care. That means taking an intellectual interest in understanding the various applications and examples of how care has changed the world for the better. There are many credible role-models who have had extraordinary spiritual experiences of caring for others. I've personally found much inspiration from their contributions. Gaining a variety of knowledge from sources of care has clarified some elementary philosophy to me: central to all service industries is the fine art of true human connection. This seems obvious, yes, but it is so profoundly deep that few will ever discover 'it' in their lifetimes. 'It' is the shared added value for all concerned. Shared added value is expressed via gratitude for being able to acknowledge others. By remaining aware within your present situation, your holistic observations will incorporate intense sensory inputs, attentive environmental observations, and intermitted mental spaciousness. In other words, you cannot truly and openly care with thoughts. Thoughts already predispose you to serve your own ego. Your ego only serves itself, period. Even if you care, if you do something 'good', for the sake of getting something out of it, subliminal conditions are attached. Such is the work of the ego, which of course is absolutely necessary in the productive world.

So, relating empathetically to others' needs requires us to become aware of our preconditioned minds. Ideally we should also have learnt from others 'care factor' examples within various socio-demographic environments. For us to act in a truly caring manner, we firstly need to recognise the ego's involvement, and not try to avoid it. Secondly we need to realise the added value we can bestow, as well as the value of lessening others' suffering or discomfort. Thirdly, we need to realise the crucial role that gratitude contributes to our mindsets, being able to share deeply with others. We should endeavour to make caring a way of life. Thus, when you become practiced in the awareness of care, and combine it with gratitude, inertia ceases to exist.

## The philosophy of giving and serving

Does caring demand sacrifice from us? For those in the industry it often feels like an enormous sacrifice on some personal level is inevitable. This is especially so when considering the frequent thankless efforts and long stressful service hours demanded by our companies and customers. What do we understand by 'sacrifice'? While it seems obvious, with health and emergency personnel working 24/7 under dire circumstances, how does it relate to the hospitality industry? We can conceptualise sacrifice as something we need to give up, a price that needs to be paid. This, once again, causes some constituent of inertia, where the pain versus pleasure ratio is troublesome to our mindset. We often tend to focus on things we have to give up, therefore on what we lose. This naturally becomes the foremost thought that enters our minds, as fear threatens the ego. Contiguous thoughts then say to us, 'this shouldn't be happening to me, I'm not being utilised to my full potential. Why am I even doing this?!'

In disasters that involve natural or man-made catastrophes, we have ample evidence that there's much caring going around. We see this especially where many people (usually more than expected) rise up to the occasion, volunteer to assist others in need in the most amazing ways. The compassion shown is often overwhelming, and does much to restore one's faith in basic human nature. This begs the question: why aren't we able to generate this element of care towards our everyday lives and work environments? Do we really need catastrophes to bring out our compassionate selves? I would say not, as we have ample examples of people everywhere that perform selfless and committed service duties by their own will. We have many excellent examples that are represented across generations, vocations and income levels of communities. Voluntary service is a fantastic indicator of a person's motivation to contribute, regardless of the benefits expected. Being willing to work for no pay is commendable indeed; however, frequently some form of benefit is present, either to the participants or the recipients. Though the more selfless a task becomes, and the less individual recognition is to be realised from it, the more altruistic contributions to others become. In some way, we can recognise that this is the theoretical shift where commercial value gradually transforms into spiritual value.

It's often difficult to serve those who are rude to us without any biased thoughts and emotions. However, it is useful to stay focused on the task that needs to be done, and the fact that effective outcomes are reliant on your approach to the 'care factor'. The undesirable behaviour of another is most often not directed toward you as a person, but is rather an emotional outlet of their frustration. Either it's their frustration at the situation, or else a reflection of their own unresolved issues. By being open-minded and tolerant of others' frustrations, we are effectively able to moderate the perpetuating reactions that might follow. As we have seen, staying mentally centred by noticing any thoughts or judgement passing through our minds makes them effectually powerless. Your ego would like to tell you that these frustrated reactions from the guest are about you and your incompetence. Intellectually, we believe that someone is attacking our being and identity, therefore threatening all we believe about ourselves.

Realise here that you are not your thoughts or actions. You are also not your performance, or your perceived worth to others. What you do, or don't do, is of no concern to the self. What is of concern for the self is being present with what is happening now. The self can only express itself through the present moment. This is the only really effective state of mind that transcends ego reactions, such as dealing with others' offensive behaviour. When you attend to others with awareness, it's unconditional, and you forfeit your made-up identity. It becomes truly liberating for your mind, as your real self cannot be affected or diminished in any way.

There are few things in life as valuable as 'random acts of kindnesses'. We are most pleasantly surprised by spontaneous actions that show that people care. Especially when we know there isn't anything in their behaviour that is motivated toward their gain. In our industry, the most memorable of service encounters are created with this principle in mind: the honest, attentive service, without obvious benefit to the server, shows real care. However, I'm not naïve. I do appreciate there's always some form of benefit involved; it could even be as subtle as feeling good about oneself. However, when we care without due benefit, it becomes pure, beautiful, and glorious. It takes on a basic, but highly spiritual dimension. The recipient most likely will be overwhelmed, and humbled that someone else could find deep value in them.

On the other hand, when one feels obliged to perform an action for someone in order to be rewarded, it reduces that spontaneity and value considerably. Therefore, to keep the value of caring 'random' and 'spontaneous', we once again need to come from a mindset that is empty of thought. This implies being non-judgemental, with no preconceived ideas about ourselves, and not consumed by what we would like to get out of it. Practically of course this is virtually impossible to achieve all the time, though with the right mindset we will be able to embrace more such random acts as they appear. When we give our full attention to our subject, and remain highly aware of our thought patterns, we are able to act more spontaneously when the opportunity arises.

Leaders need to be servants. Serving others is effectively leading their necessary actions towards determined goals. Strong leadership is positively influencing others to participate in the mutual serving of specified goals. You cannot be a leader without serving. Service is care 'actioned'. Leaders are required to lead the action, and thus caring greatly about others. They serve a greater purpose than themselves. Not only is this basic to all human beings, but it's essential for leadership. Frequently, leaders aren't the ideal role-models they are frequently seen as. Their ulterior motives are often suspect, enhanced with redundant skills. As a subordinate you often suspect there's some basic ingredient missing. However, there are many examples of fine leaders out there, who tirelessly serve and enrich others' lives beyond their own. Thus, we need to remember that true service, and especially hospitality, essentially is a noble profession that applies a duty of care toward all of humanity.

## Social confirmation

Ignorance is often incorrectly interpreted as stupidity; however, it should rather be seen as having a one-dimensional intelligence. Many intelligent people are ignorant, as they know a lot about a small number of things. However, they may remain narrow-minded in their self-knowledge, therefore lacking in real wisdom. The wise normally acknowledge that they don't know it all, and are not afraid to admit it. Actually, the more they get to know, the more they know that they don't know. In contrast, those who have a little knowledge are frequently the most arrogant about their insight. How ironic is that? Thus general ignorance is rife, especially when considering the universal mindset. Our modern consumerist society clearly reflects our inability to separate ourselves from our thoughts. Most people aren't aware of this at all, believing that their thoughts are who they are. They believe that their true identities are those that have been bestowed upon them by others. With time and maturity, we also realise that we can experiment and create our own custom-made identities at will, regardless of past history. In fact, you are able to reinvent yourself numerous times exactly how you would like others to see you! With enough resources, social media followers and social confirmation, it's up to you who you would like to be. You have the ability to play numerous roles at the same time. If your mind is completely consumed by the simultaneous roles, you may believe that you are these numerous 'people'. This could further evolve into the mental disorder of schizophrenia. Relatively, all people have some degree of mental disorder, depending on their awareness of it. The increasing degree of the disorder is usually directly related to a decreasing level of awareness.

However, when you feel the need to reinvent yourself, by definition you have not found comfort within your unchanging 'self', your core being. Because your core being cannot change, it's eternal and perfect already. Thus any empirical changes made on a pragmatic level are role-based. Who you really are, and who you portray to yourself and the world are very different. This is clearly evident in the astounding variety of roles we take on during our lives. Each of these roles has their own thought processes that constantly bombard and restrict us to specific roles and situations. This inherent inconsistency, between how the world converses with us and what we are supposed to be, is again evident from the myriad attached labels. Notice also the changing stories that define our existence from when we were born. So in understanding this, take it from me that social confirmation is not going to give you anything more than worldly expectations. Accept that we are obliged to fulfil our roles for the sake of others' beliefs. For this privilege we have socio-cultural structures, rules and conventions to guide us toward a productive and socially acceptable life. See it for what it is. It's best to adhere to its dynamics. It's also the right thing to do. However, your higher values and sense of 'self' should not be derived from social confirmation. You need to walk your own path to become aware of the true meaning of living, the value of care, and your purpose. Otherwise, you will undoubtedly remain ignorant.

With time, if you remain dedicated to intensifying your exploration into serving humanity with an intention to care, you will notice many people along the way with deep-seated causes of suffering. Besides the occurrence of tragic events, often people mistake their thoughts of suffering for reality. This effectively becomes a double-whammy, where suffering is experienced twice: once as an actual event, and then again in their minds. What they so intensely experience as mental pain is how they believe the world actually is. We all are prone to this as our minds are programmed accordingly. Nevertheless, with awareness we are also able to look outside our thoughts and realise we are able to objectify our minds. We can see the world for what it is, and that it can't inherently be different. It is what it is.

Acceptance brings the necessary non-resistance needed to deal with suffering. In times when we need to connect with suffering people, it's helpful to realise that their distorted view of reality can be alleviated. However, if you continue to believe that all the suffering you experience is representative of what is really happening, then no one will convince you otherwise. Sustaining such a closed mindset, you may take cues from your environment and others' personas to further convince you. Distort that further with a dose of prejudiced thoughts, and then add some justification from previously held beliefs. This will result in a suffering cocktail of mental toxins that filters out the natural light of awareness. Discontented behaviour is contagious, as troubled mindsets can easily be perpetuated. The cycle of discontent then carries on, until it eventually self-destructs or gets halted in its tracks. Obviously the latter is preferred, as degenerate energies from others have dire consequences. However, showing unconditional and impartial attention to others who are suffering often remedies the situation and displays trust. That way we show our willingness to move closer to recognising the being of another. Showing intimacy isn't weakness, it requires courage. We need courage to show trust regardless of others' expectations. By trusting others, we rejoice in their intrinsic worth. The act of recognising others' intrinsic worth curbs competitiveness, envy and jealousy. This leads to social confirmation at the highest level: the ability to empathise, trust unconditionally, and alleviate the suffering of others.

## Ambitions = self-care + drive

It's a wonderful quest to follow ambitions. We utilise our minds to the optimum to achieve the ultimate quests. It's true that whatever we would like to become in terms of the roles we play, we are able to. We are extraordinary gifted beings who can shape much of our destiny by design, and alter our behaviour and identity as required. Much of what we face during our worldly challenges demands courage and fortitude. For this we need suitable mental tools, and the ego provides us with the means to do so. We can conceptualise ambition as a form of 'self-care', synergised with a healthy dose of ego for 'drive'. In pursuing goals to improve our wellbeing and lifestyles, it is natural to plan for, and incorporate, ambitious endeavours. It's rather excessively Stoic if we decide to live our lives as monks in a consumer society, and ignore the fruits of modern life. Yes, there are few among us that do this; however, thankfully, it's not a prerequisite to gaining a proper perspective on your life's purpose. Ambitions are good for sustained motivation, as they usually require clearly defined objectives. Clarity on matters of achievement can, in turn, make your purpose unambiguous. Objectives necessitate the pursuit of strategies with specific tasks to be accomplished in a given timeframe. Ambitions tend to come alive with a written plan, which entails incremental minor achievements toward larger goals. Ambitions therefore have the means to consistently improve our performances by combining ego (drive) with the regulation of our mindsets (self-care) to perform at an increased level.

However, there's another darker side to ambition. Excessive ambition has the ability to be detrimental to you, and likewise, have an adverse effect on others. Competitiveness is a double-edged sword, which can be utilised to support ambition, as well as to further selfish endeavours. There are many discreet ways to get ahead in the workplace without 'selling your soul' in the process. Intent is notable here, as it should honour the development of your hospitable mindset. Whenever your values are clearly underpinning what you would like to achieve (goals), then your intentions will inevitably be aligned accordingly. It's often not 'what' you do, but 'how' you do it, that creates a worthy ambition. Whenever you devalue the worth of others in your work relationships, or consciously corrupt processes in order to increase power at someone else's cost, then ambition becomes a self-serving weapon of mass destruction. Nobody benefits in the end, even though it might bring you short-term attainment. It's inevitable that eventually all excessively ambitious endeavours will be morally contaminated in some way.

Within the competitive nature of the business environment much of these behaviours and actions might persist, or even be encouraged to further company objectives. Mindfulness is required to prevent such a competitive culture becoming your own paradigm. When fully engaged within your work life it becomes easy to lose your sense of self for the sake of the collective delusional mindset. Company values become personal values, and the role you persist in playing is scripted by the directive institution. Though it might promise many alluring rewards, it would be prudent to seriously reflect upon your purpose, and what really matters to you. The collective cultural environment is certainly very seductive, especially when the majority's values are pretty much aligned. It is natural for an ambitious employee to use systems and other means contained within the company culture to their advantage as much as possible, and to the greatest effect. However, a wise mindset remains aware of the pitfalls and challenges to the general delusional consensus. A majority, consensual or democratic system doesn't mean necessarily that it's right, true or just.

However, critical incidents have a tendency to challenge delusional perceptions. Critical incidents will certainly happen sooner or later when collective social forces aren't in harmony. For every action, there's a reaction, and all events in the universe are inextricably connected. We are mostly unconsciously aware of this fact. Therefore it's advisable to appreciate the consequences of our choices, and the effect ambitious choices have on our lives and careers. Significant to the hospitable mindset is the consideration of the 'determination' paradox: to what degree do we concern ourselves with controlling our life situations in general, and especially our ambitions?

Control presumes restrictions, which doesn't bode well for the flexibility required in any dynamic environment. As with our purpose, an initial ambition path needs to be articulated, as it will form part of our career strategies. However, the dogmatic pursuit of any goal is void of spontaneous and opportunistic quality. Life and career aren't about getting somewhere. You'll get there anyway, as the end is the same for all. As the cliché goes, it's about the journey, which means every waking moment you experience in the present time. Therefore, with the path (or general direction) established, we can pursue all that work can offer at the given moment. This approach assumes acceptance of our current circumstances as it presents itself to us. This implies that the determinist approach is futile in controlling our lives and career ambitions. However, this is once again contradictory to having the human ability to choose. We choose whatever apparent knowledge is present at the moment of decision. Every decision we make has a consequence. Therefore it has future outcomes, even though the decision can only be made in the present. This gives us the illusion of control. Thus, if controlling your future is an illusion, your future path is highly dependent on the outcomes of your present decisions and actions. For the highly ambitious amongst you the message should be clear: do as well as you can presently, aligned to a hospitable mind. The result will take care of itself.

## Empathy, sympathy, pity and compassion

Empathy is generally seen as being in touch with, or putting yourself in, someone else's emotional position. By tapping into someone else's emotions, it can be seen as a more direct path to predicting others' behaviour. Empathy also gives valuable information about a situation. It's a key ingredient in the realisation of the hospitable mind, as a nurturing factor that requires the hospitality professional to soften their social approach. It provides the opportunity for us to gain trust for that essential sense of shared connectedness. Empathy is further seen as a soft skill that needs to be approached with care and responsibility, especially as some unscrupulous people may use coercive or manipulative behaviours on vulnerable recipients for their own selfish benefits. Manipulative behaviour in business is often insincere and scripted; something which I call 'commercially-inspired interest'. This latter concept is when people are largely motivated by commercial benefit whenever they show care to others, expressed with an apparent interest in others' wellbeing. To the receptive customer, this is all too familiar. It's so commonplace that it's often acceptable, as the transactional nature of the interaction is blatantly at the forefront of the process. It cheapens the human connection. However, for the truly effective hospitable mind, this should be of secondary importance as we continue the need to truly connect. The hospitable approach directs service endeavours not for any selfish reason, but essentially for the recognition and acknowledgement of fellow sentient human beings. Empathy is a natural by-product when a mindset is attentive to not expecting benefit from service functions. Benefit might be part of the transactional process; however, through awareness the mindset is able to focus merely on the being, and separate out the commercial aspect.

Empathy is very different from sympathy, as empathy doesn't invite the involvement of emotions. One separates one's own feelings from someone else's. Nevertheless, we maintain resonance with their situation and feelings. If we find their distress or discomfort unpalatable, we may turn defensive and not function in the present as we should. Sympathy, on the other hand, reflects concern and expresses a desire to lessen suffering. This is much less commonly conducted within the workplace unless a closer personal connection has been established. With awareness, we naturally develop a fair sense of balance as to the type of behaviour that will be most appropriate to provide the best possible service for our customers.

Pity has elements of sadness and humiliation present in it. As a behaviour, it has no real place within the hospitable mind, as humiliation is an alienation of the principles of uniformity and non-judgement. Seeing any other person as beneath you (or even essentially different) has no value in service to others. It's demeaning and creates more barriers, not less. Seeing anyone as different to us essentially demonstrates that you are only looking at people superficially. Essentially, they only mean something to you if they can contribute to your world. Their value is deemed purely pragmatic. If they suit your means to an end, they receive your nod to go ahead and then should behave as you would expect them to. How presumptuous!

Becoming aware of the temporary nature of all that concerns us within our jobs and lives makes one realise that any apparent thoughts, feelings, and perceptions are fleeting. Any occurrence or object in this world is constantly changing. All appears and then disappears, with brief interludes that may last seconds, or millions of years. These cycles of life and death happen without exception. One cannot help but be awestruck. However, we too often don't realise this, and thus fall into the mind's trap of thinking that whatever is thought, is real. When we theoretically label people or things, we necessarily separate and categorise. We create divisions and silos in our minds, and unfortunately that's how we think things are in reality. However, when we break down the boundaries between all earthy beings, we necessarily find ourselves within the realm of real compassion.

By understanding the trait of compassion, we need to put two virtues at the forefront in our mindset. The first virtue in developing the trait of compassion is a sincere feeling of concern for another. We then recognise the obvious or inherent suffering in another, and as with empathy and sympathy, identify and feel their pain or discomfort. The second virtue is 'love'. Not the romantic emotion of love so commonly described. This type of love is more fundamental to the core of our being. It's extremely closely linked to the traits of appreciation and gratitude. It's simultaneously experienced inward and outward. The best way I can describe it, is that it's an intense mixture of being fully present, with heightened attention and all-round peripheral awareness. It's like being awed by everything that you can perceive with all of your senses. It can be directed to any person or object, even any situation, albeit with focussed attention.

## Why the effort to really care?

To manifest our caring mindset we need to assimilate all the theories, viewpoints and example that have been discussed so far, and make them real to us. When connecting to others, we consciously shouldn't think of anything, we shouldn't feel any emotion. Realise that any preconceived thoughts and emotions are biased. Being biased restricts true connection. Thoughts will be there, no doubt, but you should simply notice them, and not give them any more time of day. When you notice your thoughts, you become aware that you are not your mind, and most importantly, that the contents of the mind do not define you. In fact, it becomes a virtual stage of play-acting to which you are the silent audience of one, who doesn't applaud during the performance. You just silently appreciate it. Become intensely aware of your core being, your true 'self', and focus that part toward your subject. Give attention without thought to the subject. You look at it, him, or her without labelling. Practice looking without thought. Just looking, just listening, just smelling, physically feeling, and just tasting, all without giving it a thought, category, or label. With no thought obscuring the receiving of sensations, you receive it wholly and share with it fully. This exercise isn't exactly intuitive, as we adhere much too easily to our minds' messages. However this awareness needs to be first realised, then consistently practiced to be of any use. With time and continued practice, we will find that we will more frequently become openly aware, and for longer periods, no matter what the situation is or person we are facing.

Isn't it counterintuitive not to think? Our survival instincts definitely say 'think!' when we get into stressful or challenging situations. However, we know that we are most effective when thoughts are banished, and focus is pin-sharp on the task at hand. This is the reason we practice some technical skills thousands of times: not to think, not to contemplate, not to remember the steps, but to act effectively in a few seconds, with grace, influence and focus. An example we could all relate to is driving a car: when most actions have been subconsciously mastered, this clears the mind for real evasive action when personal safety is threatened. Therefore, when learning becomes part of you, it appears as and when you need it, and especially when you are being honest with yourself in terms of mastering the necessary skills. How can skills not appear when they have been extensively practiced, incorporated within your purpose, values and your essential 'self'? When you truly do communication without thinking, without evaluating, it becomes part of you. Then it becomes you. True learning can be surprising when it emerges. It happens when you 'do by not doing', by allowing the context of 'now' to happen. It is total acceptance of being in the moment, without pretence, prejudice, pretext, or precept.

However, when we are more concerned with ourselves, we become vulnerable to all extreme behaviour outside us as well. Our excessive ego blows up our reactive thoughts and feelings so that it undermines any courage to remedy the situation at hand. It creates fear, and fear manifests in inertia or inaction. Caring means directing our attention to others, not ourselves, and making it a life-long habit. Directing our 'self' outward needs simultaneous courage and humility, which presents us with an apparent oxymoron. Being humble doesn't mean being subservient. Quite to the contrary, it depicts quiet confidence. Being humble is simply noticing the sameness in everybody, that no person is superior or inferior to another. It's a highly underrated quality within the industry, especially within the corporate notions of being shrewd or ambitious. People who are aware of these qualities will appreciate them in the work environment. Even the people who readily accept egotistical traits from their colleagues will find the holistic hospitable mindset refreshing, and will prefer such an approach to foster close role-relations. The single most quoted reason for employees leaving, getting fired, or staying happily employed, is directly correlated to their personal work relationships. This again, suggests you should be caring towards others.

Suffering, self-destruction, despair, and anger have dire consequences for all. Feeling someone's anger can make us angry as well. We then similarly suffer, and in the process we close ourselves up, distance ourselves by putting up our own barrier of anger. We prefer then not to be caring; it makes us feel weak and vulnerable. We want to overly assert ourselves, as we are feeling threatened. We don't want to feel someone else's hurt. We turn into ourselves, thereby listening loud and clear to the cries of our egos saying, 'the audacity of this person to accuse me!' We naturally feel we need to protect ourselves, to affirm that it's not our fault. We try to project, and rid ourselves of any blame. We feel as though these nasty directives from others intrude on our identities. We may even feel as though our entire identity is under threat. Others' behaviour shouldn't moderate our behaviour towards them. As long as we remain aware of our 'caring' purpose, it works. Care as a core value works at a fundamental level where thoughts don't play a role. An appropriate example is that of an unprejudiced doctor and a demanding patient. The doctor sees her role in light of the professional values she accepted when entering her occupation, swearing an oath to care for others, no matter what the circumstances. Even though the doctor might reprimand the difficult patient for uncouth behaviour, she will diligently behave from a value system of compassion and care.

Within our work environments, as in life, we often see people who behave unkindly. Instead of attaching thoughts and emotions to a mind-manufactured label that is demeaning, notice your innate urge to do so. Then move on without thought. How do we effectively do this? The first and easiest method is to refuse to 'label'. Don't try and theorise what you've just seen or heard. See it with a 'no-mind'. This can be done with some dispersion of the vision the initial thought brings. Dispersing the vision or perception can be done either by zoning in with added undivided attention, or zoning out to a more peripheral view. This difference in dimension will trigger awareness in the mind-space created. Space offers a brief silence to recuperate your centre of being. If you are already caught in a fully formed thought, notice and let it pass. It will disappear unless you hold on to it, or regurgitate it in your mind. Noticing it passing by will be strengthened by the thought that it has happened, and like spilled milk, it's a now useless entity. It presents no further benefit to you, or anyone else.

See unkind people rather as ignorant, as those who don't realise that essentially all people are the same. Ignorance is bliss in some sense, as not knowing is like fish in water: they only realise what water is once they have been removed or distanced from it. They have been so totally immersed within the theoretical realm of their minds that they have not realised their shared true nature with all beings. Awareness doesn't require us to turn a blind eye to bad behaviour. When we are centred and present, we are able to attend to the task at hand with attention, confidence and fortitude. The pure motivation to care comes through us and leads us to act, ending others' discomfort or suffering, even if by force. Care is a gentle and virtuous attribute that is crucial to the hospitable mind.

Searching for a purpose, in life and career, presents us with a contradiction in terms. Presupposing a purpose is to stipulate that it should be searched for. It assumes that one needs to attain and summarily hold on to it. Unfortunately it doesn't quite work that way. We cannot search for what is already present within us. We cannot notice that the answer is already known. As the Zen riddle states, 'when you seek it, you cannot find it'; in the same way, we also cannot see what already surrounds us. Like that fish that's unconscious of the water they swim in, we are also unaware that we are already wholly emerged in purpose. That purpose has everything to do with care. Care for us, for others, for the fauna and the flora, and for Mother Earth. Most of us just don't realise it.

## CHAPTER 5

# Presenting yourself: do you have courage, or do you have fear?

*"I am not what you think I am. You are what you think I am."*

Sumayya Iftekhar

## First impressions do count, unfortunately

Our dispositions, how we approach others as a physical and energy presence, are significant in effective communication. It is quite incredible what detailed information the human senses can pick up from people communicating with us, not just directly, but also subconsciously. Much research has been done on this phenomenon. When others initially approach us, our sensory awareness and subliminal senses receive the immediate stimuli that are transmitted. These stimuli are subsequently decoded within our minds, which categorises them according to our thoughts, feelings, perceptions, and historical paradigms. Reportedly, our initial impressions are already formed within seconds of someone's approach. However we would like to deny it, first impressions count as important 'moments of truth', as they represent your best chance of creating a great first impression in hospitality. The obvious way to rise to the occasion is being as welcoming, caring, comforting and helpful as possible. With first impressions, it's all about getting it right initially. If by chance you don't get it right the first time round, it's certainly going to be much more difficult at a later stage. However, it's never too late to make a good impression; maybe not a first, but perhaps a good second impression. This presumes that recovery of initial service failure is challenging but indeed possible, and certainly most advisable.

## Smiling as a 'commodity'?

At risk of assuming the importance of the most basic and undervalued skill of hospitality, one should notice that a simple smile goes a long way. A sincere smile can most likely alleviate any other service deficiencies you might have. It is certainly the simplest of actions that require the least effort; however, it's most frequently taken for granted. Amazingly, it's often not taught, or managed in its rightful place within the service industry. Reportedly, for humans there are fewer muscles needed to smile than to frown, yet we tend to see indifferent facial expressions more often than not. As can be expected, some cultures are naturally friendlier and therefore more prone to smiling than others, regardless of their economic or technological advancement. Hofstede found that some cultures with high power differentiation are more formal, thus they are also less likely to connect with a smile. Culture certainly has an impact on the acceptable recognition of others, but so too does the individual's socio-demographic make-up. Smiling as a basic human trait begs acknowledgement, solicits reciprocal warmth, and shares a sense of 'being-ness'. It's a wonderfully dynamic illustration of how souls meet, especially as facilitated through the eyes. No wonder they say that the eyes are 'the windows to the soul'.

Personally I've explored the reactive effect of smiling at strangers. The reason why I embarked on such a quest was rather personal. Presenting myself to others with a smile made me feel more in touch with them, more comfortable and confident. Such a smile would also make me feel happier, relax my facial muscles, and had the added advantage of making me more aware of my environment. Smiling drew my attention outward, outside my mind. I found that I could stay intensely in the present moment as long as the focus was on keeping my smile intact. Simultaneously, I was less bothered by distracting thoughts as I was concentrated outwardly. Finding this method especially useful, I feel I have to share it with my fellow hospitality practitioners, for it might be of value within the service environment.

However, please note that this 'half-smile' that I advocate has substance. Genuineness cannot be faked. The smile cannot be overplayed, forced, or acted. Anyone will notice a fake smile, either consciously or unconsciously. The only way that you can achieve a genuine smile is by deeply communicating that smile through your eyes, transmitting the warm feeling that emanates from within, and a shared feeling of connection. Not to complicate matters, but you should try not thinking. Refrain from labelling, feeling an emotion or jumping to any conclusions. I guarantee the results will surprise you. The result that stood out with my exploratory quest was the 'mirror image' reaction from others who noticed my smile. Most of these were strangers and they mirrored my behaviour. Mostly my demeanour was being reflected back to me, which was hugely encouraging. As my connection with some of them further developed, other positive results included increased depth of interaction, increased mutual listening and enhanced understanding.

Thus I advise you to practice your relationships accompanied with a smile. You need to habitually use it to remain consistently effective in connecting to others. Reflect on how it works for you; notice the triggers required to bring it spontaneously to your face as required. Do it with the true genuineness your customers deserve. It's not by chance that the Buddha was famously known for a peaceful smile whilst meditating, which epitomises the peace within him. Another famous smile is Da Vinci's Mona Lisa, and her smile has been fiercely debated for centuries. A smile's attraction is undeniable. It has the ability to soften our apparent differences and entice human beings to connect with each other. It's truly a superpower that is essential to cultivate within the hospitable mind.

## Relationships with colleagues

Conducting yourself properly in relation to workplace peers can be challenging, as many academics and professionals have illustrated with their life's contributions to the science of psycho-social factors. The scope of knowledge in these behavioural sciences is immense. However, if it comes to cultivating the hospitable mindset, I keep issues elementary so as to be clearly understood and practical to the industry. Quality relationships with your colleagues are crucial for progressing in your career and work environment. There's just no getting around it. It determines your internal mental health and your external social effectiveness. Central to attaining and sustaining good relationships with colleagues is the fundamental value of trust.

Trust is the absence of fear. Fear causes inertia, and restricts constructive and creative thinking. Fear often causes inaction. However trust is not an absolute quality, where all uncertainties fall away. There's always some level of trust present within our minds, from the utmost trust we have with complete confidence, to a total lack of trust coupled with severe suspicion. Levels of trust relate directly to our paradigms and associated histories. Trust is not just associated with our historical beliefs, but is also reflected as an attitude. This attitude leads to actionable decisions, whereby we become trusting in what we're about to choose. For example, we could choose to go along with someone's authority (therefore trusting their leading capacity to guide us), or else choose to rather follow our own way (instead trusting our own opinion). The people we trust most have the most influence in our lives and careers. Thus, trust is an essential enabler of speed, effectiveness, and open communication between people. We generally know that trust enhances all the necessary virtues in work and life.

However, we need to assess the significance of trust in cultivating our hospitable mindsets. The popular notion is that some people are worthy of trust, and some aren't. It's a cliché that trust is earned: that it works like a bank account, where more should be deposited than withdrawn. Unfortunately this is a fallacy. It's an oversimplification of a dynamic trait. Our preconceived thoughts are highly active when it comes to the trust issue, as all our previous biased and justified decisions, based on past experiences, come flooding back. Trust can only be based on the limited information that we subjectively process from our minds, thus it's already inherently restricted and partial. Add to that our limited perceptions of current reality and the information processed potentially has consequential flaws. Even if we were accurate with our trust assessment, who can say similar results will arise at different times, places and circumstances? Besides, in hospitality we rarely know our customers well enough to determine any level of 'conventional' trust. However, trust on a basic level is crucial to show that we care for, and respect them. This similar basic trust should be levelled toward all we interact with, not just colleagues. Where there's doubt, there's usually suspicion. However, I would urge you to adopt an attitude of 'give them the benefit of the doubt' always, as this will work out more in your favour than you might expect. With this I don't mean you should be a feeble pushover or act as a doormat for someone to potentially mistreat. No, I mean that you should realise that you don't have to have total insight of the other person, their personal circumstances, mindset, or history to trust them sufficiently. Trust given already shows another that you have confidence in them, that you care, and that you share a connection. Without trust, no extent of superficial niceties will convince them. It's your challenge to build trust, to truly connect. Whatever effort you make in accomplishing this will reward you many times over.

Of course to build trust, you need to trust yourself as well. This comes from accepting yourself, warts and all. Acceptance of yourself requires knowing how your mindset functions, the extent to which you are aware of the relationship between your ego and your thoughts. Your values and beliefs underpin much of your thought processes, and determine much of the emotional comfort levels you experience daily. Remember that the 'self' remains impartial to mental processes, and lets the mind get on with the job it does best: progressing thoughts effectively within the empirical world. The result is self-trust. Self-trust is the quality relationship of your 'self' with your conscious mind.

Can we trust our thoughts? The short answer is no. However, we can trust our thoughts to do exactly what they are supposed to do – effectively giving us the tools to lead our lives with purpose and intent. We cannot, nevertheless, expect our thoughts to be real. They are figments of the imagination, changeable, distorted, and dependent on context. They become, in a nutshell, what we want them to be. Thus they are tools that are used for either our benefit or hindrance. That we alone decide. So, once we are able to observe our mind as an independent object from our 'selves', then we are able to trust the thoughts that arise; not for empirical accuracy, but for discretionary practical value. Thoughts become very serious to us when we mistake our thoughts for our true essence. Thus, thoughts should never be taken seriously. Our thoughts should rather be used to build self-credibility at every available opportunity, to enhance one's self-confidence and discipline. Self-credibility comes to you when you stay true to yourself, trusting your motives and aligning your actions accordingly. You then improve your competence in managing yourself effectively. This creates the necessary open mind for truly trusting ourselves and others.

## Extrovert versus introvert

Interestingly, research shows that being an introvert doesn't present any significant handicaps to providing quality guest service, or a liability in creating an outstanding hospitable mindset. In fact, being more inner-mind focused and reflective increases awareness and keeps you more directly in touch with your emotions, with a higher level of controlled thoughts. Often we find that extroverts react before thinking or contemplating what they are about to do or say. Such action-orientated service approaches might shortcut or forfeit the depth of social connection necessary for excellent hospitality. However, extraversion makes it somewhat easier to relate to strangers with confidence and spontaneity. We can thus be sure that most people have variable proportions of both approaches. However dominant your natural tendencies might be, we are consciously able to alter our behaviour according to our changing mindset and related situations.

For example, I have always been regarded as an introvert, and during childhood especially seen as somewhat shy and underachieving. Once out working, the lessons of life's hard knocks gave me the proverbial kick in the backside. Fondly remembered was the opportunity to perform as 'master of ceremony' at a friend's wedding. I accepted the challenge and failed miserably. The story would've ended there, were it not for a five-year-old girl poking me in the stomach whilst I was leaving the ceremony, mortified, saying 'Hey mister, I think you're funny!' Well, that fan-base of one enticed me to do the same again with multiple weddings after, to much more encouraging effect.

I've since become a lecturer, and now I continuously speak to audiences for a living. The net effect is that I can summon my 'extraversion' when required, and when on stage I perform quite well and, most importantly, enjoy it. The same goes for facing customers or strangers: I feel it takes more of my energy resources than most other people. I feel my attention and listening levels need to be consciously heightened to be fully on form. When I have to perform at my best, a session of quiet meditation beforehand helps tremendously to enhance clarity of mind and boost my energy levels. In fact, I have found that many mini-meditational moments throughout the day have often enhanced my attention and focus when needed. Once I was prepared, I found that I wouldn't have to think or fret, and I could just be in the present moment with whatever is needed from me, without expectations. With awareness, actions become effortless and spontaneous. I have found that a quiet awareness will enhance your approach to customers, and contribute towards cultivating your hospitable mind.

## Dichotomy of expectations

I'm quite critical of mind, and a known cynic in some circles. In the past, on some occasions, I have had an appetite for playing devil's advocate, where intentionally I lure others into arguments or get them to react passionately. My ego used to find some kind of satisfaction in seeing people get heated about what they believe in. However, this was all playacting to me. I do now realise that mind games could be hurtful to others, yet in the past I did sometimes persist for my own selfish gains. I enjoyed creating chaotic conversations, using frivolous theories one could hardly imagine possible. I realised then that the mind is truly an astounding and ingenious tool to play with. An added benefit was that I became more fascinated by the fickleness of the human mind. The mind truly does exactly what is asked of it, and we are often deeply immersed in its seductive turmoil of thoughts. We just don't realise it. Challenging others' expectations of me to behave in a certain way resulted in me become socially obstinate and tedious to others. I wanted to assert myself differently to convention. I must admit it was my poor attempt to gain much needed respect and acknowledgment. Additionally, from feedback I've learnt that being critical, without being constructive, does exactly the same damage. It asserts to others that only your judgement matters, and that they are inevitably wrong, bad or unacceptable. Conversely, constructive feedback is providing empathetic guidance aimed at improving their behaviour or performance. The ego factor is taken out of it. The self-assertion dissipates, and the focus moves onto the other person. One doesn't then persist in strengthening one's own self-image. I did eventually learn the lesson, though.

By now you have probably noticed that I'm advocating that wherever life throws at us, we shouldn't have any expectations about it. Considering and implementing this simplifies our mindsets tremendously and makes us more receptive to others' needs. We can expect the sun to rise tomorrow morning with absolute certainty, but we can be less certain we'll awake to see it. Actually, the only thing we can totally expect is what is happening in this actual moment. Then the next moment, and the next. The concept of time is highly abstract and mind-made, and the reality of it deludes our senses, unless we attend to it in real time. The only real time is present time. Thus time actually doesn't exist, and the only sliver of time's existence is the split second we notice it, whilst living in the present. Obviously that's only if we are aware of the present moment, which most often we're not. In our minds we habitually live in the past and anticipate the future, with very little time spent being aware of the 'now'.

I'm reiterating this to illustrate where expectations come in. When we expect, we project our desired outcomes about the future. We approach situations and people with an expectation of what we hope to experience. This is preconceived, thus a futile impression of what 'should' happen. When it doesn't materialise as we expect, we are disappointed, and ultimately unhappiness follows. Invariably this will happen often enough that such occurrences determine our habitual thought patterns. In turn it becomes our reality. Without awareness, we cannot envision ourselves outside of this 'reality' of the mind.

High expectations are consistently satisfied less often than low expectations. More to the point, no expectations always get satisfied. You cannot be disappointed when you have no expectations. Understand that this eradication of expectations isn't a denial of reality. In effect you are embracing the awareness of your thought origins, noticing the purpose of the expectant ego, and the self. The ideal outcome is that all experiences can then be enjoyed for what they are, as one realises that all outcomes inherently contribute value. It follows that an opportunity to be grateful then exists for all outcomes, good or bad. Thus, where there's value to benefit from, there's inevitably space generated for gratitude.

Let me tell you the secret recipe for dealing with expectations that don't turn out as we hoped for: 'fascination'. I mentioned the child-like naivety we systematically lose throughout our lives. This is shame, as we lose much of our spontaneous enthusiasm because of the innate cynicism that comes with age. However, a remedy for me that has worked well is the theoretical transformation of 'frustration' into 'fascination'. In the past, whatever expectations I've had predictably led to me judging if they were being satisfied or not. This substantially impacted on my feelings of general happiness. For example, I wanted to be noticed by management for specific contributions at work. It was a futile expectation, as it never happened. Of course I blamed others and got frustrated, and displayed some inappropriate behaviour, which didn't help matters.

Nowadays, I have changed my attitude, as I realise that acceptance and gratitude have formed a firm foundation of my values. I notice, reflect on, and then change the roots of frustration into an empowering flow of fascination. With this mindset method I concentrate on being inquisitive and amazed by the apparently challenging situation. The energy that initially came from being frustrated, alters and now flows with a more light-hearted understanding of 'what is, is'. I realise that my expectations were probably inappropriate, and not warranted. This sense of inquisitiveness brings out the child in me, and it feels natural to wonder, to remain enthusiastic, and to say, 'it doesn't really matter, I'm still okay'. Stay fascinated!

## The cause and symptoms of service

For every thorough analysis we should distinguish between cause and symptoms. Quite often we are looking at the surface of problems from the point of view of obvious symptoms, missing the deeper lying cause of the problem altogether. Often, we are not even able to define the problem clearly. However, we usually expect excellent results. A number of studies and books are dedicated to the science of service management, with many theories attempting to explain the intricacies of effective service. Here I shall attempt to distil the complex into the simple. There's a popular belief that excellent service delivery is an inherent quality we all possess. Like driving, most people do actually think that they are good at it. As an academic, I appreciate the scope and depth of service quality theory. There are many different variables at work within the service process; therefore I understand its application is much more challenging than is commonly understood.

It all starts with the question: 'why do we serve?' When we've clarified the 'why', we can get an intellectual grip on the 'how'. We should clearly see our instinctive lifetime task as service to others: including the community, organisations, loved ones, and our various personal purposes. We are often prompted to give as much service as we receive. Service becomes part of reciprocal community involvement. No organisation can do without it. Fundamentally, effective service delivery includes the following tasks: acknowledgement, attention, respect, care, connection, and gratitude. Most of these have been discussed and clarified in this book. Many of these tasks overlap in context, and many mutate throughout the service process. However, the most descriptive concept that we could gather them all in, would be 'awareness'. Being aware means we are clear on our purpose, thus why we are serving, and in what role we hope to do justice to the purpose. This could be in a leadership position, or in an operational role. Clarify and reflect on what you are doing to make others' daily lives and careers improve. Even if you are of relative unimportance in the worlds' view of stature, you are born to 'be', thus you matter far more than you generally realise. However small individual contributions might seem, they are significant in the scheme of the universe, where all things of prominence rely on the smallest of affinities. Reflect on your added value, and you will notice that service is central to all those whom you come in contact with.

If it comes to 'how' we develop fundamental service awareness, we should look deep into our psyches. Awareness not only looks outward by accepting others unconditionally as they appear. It also looks inward, by noticing to what extent the ego is progressing in strengthening its individualism. Outward awareness focusses on listening intently without thought; inwardly it clears away intruding thoughts about social context through attentive observation. Outward awareness feels the energy connection with the other, whereas inwardly we create mind-space for the unexpected. With awareness, we give ourselves enough mental space and stillness in our minds. We create space so that it can be completely filled by connecting with other beings. When we are preoccupied (observing our mobile phones, or lost within incessant thinking) we have not created space for anyone else's being. Being aware allows us to pick up subtle nuances of behaviour that others might miss. Awareness absorbs body language clearly, and it can often pre-empt others' needs before they are verbally communicated. It effectively detects what needs to be known, by already knowing. You don't need to know your customer; you already know them on the fundamental level required when you're aware. This is the formula to being truly extraordinary at serving others: a clear purpose shows 'why' and putting awareness in action shows 'how' to make it happen consistently. It's not rocket science, but it could be difficult for some to see past their common assumptions.

## Zen and the art of effort

For much of my career, and then some more in hospitality, I have struggled to apply myself at work. As mentioned before, taking the easy route with the least effort was automatic to me. I grew up quite privileged, so there wasn't really a need for personal resourcefulness. I performed poorly earlier in my studies and career, mainly because of being uncommitted to a clear purpose. I was doing silly stuff for the wrong reasons. However, as I matured in my thinking and enthusiastically explored life's many mysteries, I gained some wisdom from my many seemingly failed undertakings.

My original and rather suitable Zen-like parable comes to mind when I contemplate the art of effort: 'disguised beyond the darkened windows of a limousine the rich man stares out in silence onto a wet and windy world that seems chaotic in comparison to his opulent and comfy island of mobile serenity. He is chauffeured to important appointments, meticulously planned and timed for predetermined arrival. Alongside the limousine in the chaotic traffic congestion, pulls up a man on a bicycle, drenched from the rain and totally exposed to the surroundings. The two men look at each other. The man on the bike smiles as their eyes meet. The rich man momentarily looks at him, indifferently grimaces and looks away.'

Unfortunately, like the rich man, as we become more comfortable within our surroundings with familiar people, we become also more prone to inertia. Comfort often pacifies our desire to do something different or daring, and we tend to stick to our personal customs of known entities and thoughts. Accepting our current, often turbulent environment, warts and all like the smiling cyclist, leads to non-resistance to life's challenges. When we expose our vulnerability to others and to the unknown environmental elements, we are showing real courage in staying open-minded. Therefore we become acceptant to those circumstances we cannot control. This facilitates action. The effort is often not even consciously contemplated, thus becomes non-existent in the mind. In other words you just do it, without much thought. When you are part of the elements, you are more involved, you participate and you subsequently feel more alive.

Every time I have the privilege to get on a bicycle, I feel like I'm 13 years old. It's precious. Moving to England, it took me only one cold winter season commuting on a bicycle to wholly accept the elements, and experience the spontaneous joy a kid would have. I couldn't wait to commute on my bike! This is how you get into the moment; wherever you are, you're already actively involved. You need to be aware of how your being participates with everything around you. There's no 'putting in effort', as it has already been accomplished. It is there already. You just need to ride it out.

On the other hand, like the rich man, insulating ourselves from reality by giving ourselves a false sense of security, creates delusions. Yes, one feels more secure and comfortable within environments suited to our sense of who we are, and thus our perceived identities. We sometimes feel we need to separate ourselves from others to strengthen our ideas about ourselves. This is where distrust and fear are generated. When we feel our identities are threatened, we shrink within ourselves, and the ego rationalises it's 'us against them'. It vaporises spontaneity and openness in favour of increased critical judgement. When we judge, we do so with premeditative thought, and it blocks our willingness to become presently active. We rationalise why or why not we should be doing it, we contemplate others' actions, what might go wrong, and the dire consequences to us. Too much mental traffic slows our call to action, creates inertia, and impairs our attention. It's that simple. By the way, no rich men were harmed during the production of this book.

## Change behaviours, and attitudes will follow

To be able to work on our attitudes, we need to first alter our behaviour and habits. To see every moment as an opportunity, something afresh and new, is to look at the world like a child. Have you seen how spontaneously happy children are doing seemingly mundane things? This is until a grownup tells them 'not to', or until they have thoughts of guilt, feelings of fear, or some other restrictive conformation. Unfortunately this natural enthusiasm to life's wonders becomes muddled by restrictive social conventions, expectations, media, rules, and culture. Lots of the wow-factor gets lost as one gets older. Passion and optimism are often replaced by increased cynicism and division. So what can we do about this? Whatever society has imposed on us should be carefully dissected to see how it has influenced our mindset. What have people and institutions said about who we are to them, and how we should behave? Yes, to succeed in the workplace we need to follow certain conventions to get the job done, and to ensure that we fit in. There's no way around that. However, many of us play it safe to blend in, forgetting that we are a unique and dynamic personality, with unique abilities to further our purpose. Hence again the paradox of celebrating individualism on a mental level, but embracing unity with all other humans on a spiritual level.

How do we regain this dormant enthusiasm from childhood? The only way is to become as we once were in childhood; not in an intellectual way, but in an attitudinal way. It is indeed unfortunate that, as we become more intellectually stimulated through means of education, we also become increasingly analytical. This is, of course, very good for rationalising the world in a systematic manner; however, it has robbed us somewhat of the awe of mundane discoveries. Accordingly, the face value of things starts to mean less to us as our increasing thoughts interpret all we perceive. The spontaneity of the initial contact with reality is mostly eroded by conjuring up conceptual interpretations, categorising and labelling everything.

The French philosopher René Descartes stated, 'I think, therefore I am', which essentially demonstrates most people's belief that the mind represents the self, as they usually cannot distinguish any separation between the two during their lifetimes. We don't need to think about conceptualising something when we look, listen, taste, smell or touch something. No, we can just experience the sense without attaching a connotation to it, just like a fascinated baby would do in the first few years of its life. Imagine yourself becoming so receptive to all that is happening around you, that you are constantly 'high' on awareness. You feel all the material energies, the visual stimuli, the array of sounds reverberating, and the inseparable sense of being. It consumes your mind so much that there aren't any conscious thoughts, just awareness of being in this place and in the now. There are no distractions, worries, wishes, wants or needs. There are no expectations and there's a full acceptance of the current environment. This was just like you were so many years ago, before you had to analyse everything. Absolute bliss. This is where a wholesome attitude originates from, a place of 'no-mind'. It clears the mind palette of cluttered thought to initiate near-effortless action. This is the implicit point to Nike's famous slogan, 'just do it', where you act without preceding and contemplative thought. Thus changing your behaviour, facilitating the elimination of thought, will shape the required attitude you need to cultivate the hospitable mind.

## Being professional

As first impressions are socially important, professionalism relates to the required norms and behaviours associated with effectiveness in the industry. You, by nature of your duties, are required to present yourself in the most favourable way possible. This is not so much for your benefit (although the rewards justify the means), as for others' benefit. Customers want to be served by someone they can trust and relate to. 'Professional' can mean many things to many people, and of course, definitions and related analyses are far and widely researched. However, how the mindset is related to 'being professional' is much more basic to understand, and therefore easier to internalise. The myriad technical issues include preferred behaviour towards colleagues and customers: integrity, empathy, self-management, self-hygiene and appearance, confidence, effective and careful delivery of service, etc. There are volumes written on these subjects; however, I would like to distil it all down to a simple way of thinking.

The first question, as usual, is why? From there we can progress to the how. Essentially, professional service requires the customer to receive personal attention, recognition, authentic and effective behaviour, and value for money. To go beyond the service norm is effectively going beyond customers' expectations. This entails establishing positive surprise, which further implies that it needs to be unanticipated, thus not to customary standards. Pleasant surprises are memorable, and will most likely be talked about to others. As an example, random acts of kindness stick out in our memories as significant. Predictability is often 'boring' even though it shows consistency in standards. You can be sure that the overuse of methodological approaches to service will lead to stagnation and eventual loss of patronage. It's wringing the spontaneity out of a convivial opportunity.

Charm is often not expected; nevertheless I think all of us possess a natural charm when we are spontaneous. What one needs to accomplish with authentic service quality, is non-stereotyped behaviour, where the surprise factor eliminates customers' mental defences. To the customer, a pleasant spontaneous connection conceals any intentions, and it doesn't seem premeditated. It demonstrates a degree of vulnerability to the customer, which seems much more natural and sets a mutually tolerant tone for further communication. Without a script to act out, thus void of a pre-set mental construct, there's a sense of playfulness. We can gather without a doubt that a customer wants to feel it's all about them. They want to feel validated by getting full attention from people that care. This need for recognition and respect is common to all people. Thus, being professional is acquiring the consistent ability to provide for these needs.

How do we accomplish professionalism? As we recognised earlier, this is much easier said than done with people we are close to. However, it calls for a change of mindset to be properly professional with everybody. Besides all the technical factors that need to be in place, your mind is of utmost importance when implementing the many advisable virtues and habits. All the accumulated knowledge in the world will be of little use without effectively controlling your thoughts, or you will lapse into previous patterns of behaviour. For a start, forget about yourself and your hoarded history, as you most probably have already internalised it unconsciously from when you were born. You do not need to bring yourself into your thoughts, especially when serving someone or something else. Abstaining from general thought activity inevitably focusses your attention on the other person. Clearing your mind renders you open to receiving the other person fully with every nuance that you may be able to pick up. Your senses will be alerted, and your initial empty mind will be able to take on a request for action or reaction without restriction. You will be able to listen fully to what is said, what it should mean from their point of view, and how it's expressed. This is wholesome communication, and can only be achieved when not hindered by preconceived thoughts. Your preparation should only consist of clearing your mind and giving attention. It's as easy as that. This will ensure the necessary spontaneity and natural charm to put anyone at ease. This is basic to the art of hospitality.

CHAPTER 6:

# Mindset:
# are you embracing the hospitable way?

*"Non-resistance, non-judgement, and non-attachment are the three aspects of true freedom and enlightened living."*

Eckhart Tolle

## Cultivating the 'no-mind'

In this last chapter I would like to leave you with some concluding insights on life, your career path and the further associated psychological development needed. There are no sure remedies when the path calls for lasting happiness, in life and work. As you may appreciate, there are many pointers, and I've attempted to bring in those that I've seen work for me and the people I've been able to guide. The pointers are just that, simple indicators of a direction that can be followed, albeit on your own path, in your own time. I like simplifying life's extraordinary complexities. I like to follow modest principles, as they have a better chance of becoming part of everyday life. Rigorous analysis is good up to a point, and beyond it, the mind interferes with the really important issues. Accumulation of knowledge, understanding it, applying it and the relationship with our world is ample scope for our conscious minds. Beyond our minds we have an undiscovered vastness that few will ever recognise. This is where we see that all the information in the world has no power at all. The strangest thing is that we already have the 'key' to open the space beyond our minds. It's not something we can find somewhere else. It's already part of us, and it just needs to be realised.

We've discussed the benefits of 'no-mind'. This is an elementary but essential step into the vastness of the self, beyond the thoughts in the mind. The no-mind doesn't equate to inaction or ignorance, quite the contrary. It creates the space necessary to absorb and to be aware. It needs to be consciously practiced, and with repetition, eventually it will require no conscious thought. It will become a productive habit that opens you up to others in any challenging situation. Thus it's imperative for the cultivation of the hospitable mind. I've been fortunate in practicing martial arts for around 25 years, so I've experienced the no-mind phenomenon entrenched within the Japanese defence psyche. Once attacked, one cannot contemplate anything, either fight- or flight-related. One has to resort to immediate action, without thought. Thought slows you down, and becomes an obstacle that could lead to defeat. Similarly, being hospitable requires the least possible thought processes, mutually connecting through the available split-seconds of truth. This enables focused attention with the peripheral awareness necessary to serve the customer environment holistically. The service process is made up of intervals of no-mind and mindfulness, where subliminal awareness constantly interchanges with sensory messages, regulated by conscious emotional intelligence. Generally, by noticing mind activity it dissipates automatically. Otherwise, an intentional no-mind can be achieved by focussed attention on the person in front of you, assisted by deep even breathing, and listening intently and actively, without a thought.

## Eliminating resistance for a fascinating life in hospitality

The Buddhists have typified three 'poisons of the mind': ignorance, craving and hatred. Ignorance, as mentioned before, isn't lack of knowledge. It's being ignorant as to the true nature of the world, as opposed to our meddlesome subjective thoughts. Craving, or desire, is a further perpetuation of ideas about what we hope for in the future. It's a mental state of what we expect or wish for, but unfortunately brings no promises or guarantees. Craving means focussing on outcomes, to the detriment of present input; losing your quality involvement in the present moment. As Lao Tzu states, 'the journey of a thousand miles begins with one step'; your focus should be on the next step to take. The direction can periodically be checked; however, it should never be the sole focus. Otherwise you will not fully remember the precious and unique journey, and not enjoy its splendour and sufferings.

By resting assured that consistent steps will progress you to inevitable outcomes, internal resistance to the effort required increasingly diminishes. You will gain confidence in accepting the challenges ahead. Hatred, as the last poison, is seen as non-acceptance of yourself, of others and of the seemingly abhorrent situation you might find yourself in. Hatred, though, is seen as a strong emotion, redolent of distrust, anger and judgment, and therefore solely based on your made-up mindset. Everyone needs to effectively process life's challenges, which include others' ignorance and dire situations. Not only should you remain empathetic to the ignorance of others, but you should also not take anything that happens personally. By personally, I mean as a threat to your self-derived identity. For example, when a customer rudely accuses you of undesired behaviour, you should, as Stephen R. Covey famously stated, 'seek first to understand, then to be understood'. This means relinquishing all resistance to defending yourself. You create a deep connection by trying to fully understand the customer's point of view. It takes both awareness of your own inner state of mind, as well as being intently aware of the customer. Your own mind should be free of thought, with total non-resistance, avoiding any psychological defence. Most customers will react to this mindset with initial confusion or reciprocal acceptance. This process will effectively dissipate all conflict.

The simplest way to eradicate these poisons is to cultivate an attitude of non-resistance. Kafka wrote, 'war is the monstrous lack of imagination', which brings to light the idea that creative solutions cannot coexist with war. It means violent engagement has cut off any unifying connection we have as humans. After war, however, reflection can remedy the issues, and find solace in some peaceful resolutions. Conflict should be seen as a valuable messenger for us, a signal to give the necessary attention to a situation, without prejudice or defence. War is resistance to what 'is', which means we cannot accept the current moment. That doesn't mean we should be weak or lethargic in the face of conflict. No, it means we are more receptive to others' plight, and we don't regard defending our egos as a valid reason for conflict. Egos work on a basis of 'tit-for-tat', and defend a fragile identity at all costs, sometimes at extreme cost to oneself. Identifying with the collective mind, such as an ideology in war situations, is madness.

Being mindlessly nationalistic, or stubbornly mind-induced to a specific culture, religion or organisation, is dangerous indeed. It, by definition, separates humankind with mental and physical barriers, with corresponding discriminatory labels and categories. Conflict can be constructive and even beneficial, in that it should eventually teach us the required personal path to take, in lessening our and others' distress.

Bringing non-resistance into other parts of work and life leads to less stress and better mental health. Often when we are challenged by unforeseen daily issues, we tend to 'react' and not 'respond'. 'Reacting' means those knee-jerk thoughts and emotions that seemingly appear out of nowhere. They are those reactions that get us into trouble, as they are so instantaneous that they were not sufficiently reflected upon. Invariably, such actions are supplemented with intense emotions, which exacerbate the situation even more. 'Response' is a calmer, more rational and even-tempered reply to a situation that minimises the emotional predisposition. It effectively weakens an intense emotional situation. By being aware of our own mindset, we can deliver a calm response when needed, without feeling threatened. When the response is clear, truthful and transparent in its intention, it remedies an undesirable situation.

Wherever we might encounter resistance in our thoughts, relationships, and socio-demographic environments, we should remain aware of their impact on our own mindsets. Resistance is non-acceptance of the current situation, which is re-establishing expectations from the mind's thought processes. We want our current situation to be different, and our tumultuous thoughts dominate our experience of the dire situation. My early days in hospitality were fraught with such thoughts, especially enhanced when cleaning guests' toilets. Instead of resisting thoughts, I should have embraced the current situation fully. There I was, indeed fortunate to be in war-torn Palestinian areas, experiencing a wondrous time of my life. I was certainly getting my fair share of hospitality basics into my system. Adverse experience often acts as a high-pressure cooker; it enables the rapid awareness of purpose and gratitude. As Roger Federer famously said after his 5th Wimbledon title, 'You need a certain intensity to make it through a crucial moment'. Always be able to notice the privilege of contribution, to becoming part of something beyond yourself (even if it happens to be a toilet).

## Continuous evolution

In conclusion, the setting of goals, preferably in writing, is imperative to achieving your life's objectives. These goals should be broad 'life goals' as well as smaller, more specific ones for each role in your life. Don't allow family or other people to set your goals for you. You are in the best position to do this, and realise you only need to answer to yourself. However, don't treat your goals as the be-all or end-all. They will change as you mature, according to your shifting priorities. Don't obsess about reaching goals, as the answer to happiness is not in achieving, or gathering possessions. Concentrate on attending to the first step in achieving them, and thereafter take it one step at a time. Like a road map, yes, you certainly need to know where you are going; however, it's at your own pace and in a general direction, as you need a degree of spontaneity and flexibility to add spice to your life. Note that the direct route isn't necessarily the best.

Health is crucial for happiness. A good foundation to mental wellbeing is good physical health. This connection has been proven by countless studies. Achievement of one leads to positive development of the other. This results in improved self-discipline, and enhanced motivational levels. Make lifelong learning a habit. Self-improvement involves making and breaking habits. Gaining expert knowledge without wisdom is not enough, though; it often promises quick solutions, with flashy short-term rewards. Wisdom is deeper and much more substantial. It requires holistic and spiritual insight. Wisdom becomes a lifestyle that has real purpose, with values and virtues. Fundamental issues and methods have been discussed in this book. With constant reflection, practising these methods becomes habit. These behavioural habits become part of your mindset. With time, you should not even have to think about methods. You should be able to do it 'unconsciously', without thought, without premonition. This is the realisation of the hospitable mind.

Don't compare yourself to others. On occasion it can be motivating but most often not, because it isn't based on 'reality', only on perception. No two people are the same, and you can't compare individuals that inherently have different physical, psychological, and personality traits. 'Everyone enters the race at a different stage and runs at their own pace'. Working systematically and attentively toward your own goals is the greatest motivation booster one can get.

Practice and incorporate gratitude into your life. It is easy to take privileges for granted. Try this: for the next couple of days, consider all the resources needed that add to your experiences. Where did they come from, and who created them? What are the things that have made you what you are today? Consider the special people that have touched your life in some way. As a result, it becomes increasingly difficult to say that you have extraordinary 'troubles' or valid 'excuses' not to be the best you can be. You only fail if you quit. If progress or expectations do not go your way, then it becomes a useful and necessary learning curve.

There are three layers of sustainable self-motivation. Firstly, by finding your passion and purpose. True success is reliant on continuous goal-making and achievement, which should originate from something you enjoy doing. You can learn to enjoy it, but eventually you must enjoy it, to experience the true intrinsic rewards.

Secondly, by changing your reality. In order to cultivate the right habits to achieve success, you need to script your life's roles, manage your thoughts, manage the scene as best you can, and direct the cast as far as your influence will go. You virtually become your own director. You can learn from mistakes, or you can become defensive. It is always your choice.

Thirdly, connect to your activity. Be present, be conscious, and be in the 'now'. Nothing matters more than being present. If you are thinking of the future, or fretting about the past, you are not aware of the present. You are living in your mind, which is not life, but a construct of your own imaginary vision and thoughts of subjective perception. 'Being lost to the present moment might as well equate to not existing.' These are wise words indeed, from Eckhart Tolle. By being aware and present, you cannot help but be motivated. You absorb all that occurs with focus, attention and clarity. You move without the constraints of thought or emotion, and unconsciously you know that 'nothing else matters' in that second. An empty mind that is aware is enlightened.

## ABOUT THE AUTHOR

Dr Leon van Achterbergh is currently the Senior Professional Training Tutor and Senior Teaching Fellow at the School of Hospitality and Tourism Management, University of Surrey. His working career extends over 30 years, which includes industry experiences in retail, insurance, engineering, and hospitality. His academic career started 14 years ago, after gaining a Master's degree at the globally acclaimed Ecole hôtelière de Lausanne, in Switzerland. Subsequently he was appointed as lecturer at a global campus site in South Africa for a Dutch university, Stenden. He gained his PhD in Business Management in 2013, before relocating to the United Kingdom. Since embarking on his academic career, Dr van Achterbergh has been dedicated to provide guidance, coaching and supervision to university students with their internships, industrial placements and career development.

Services provided:
    Consultation
    Motivational Speaking
    Lectures & Workshops
    Work-based Learning for Companies
    Professional Development
    Human Resource Profiling
    Mystery Guest
    Mentoring
    Mediation

For further information and services rendered, please visit:
    thehospitablemind.org
    linkedin.com/in/lvanachterbergh/